THE HOME FRONT IN BRITAIN 1914–18: AN ARCHAEOLOGICAL HANDBOOK

Historic England

HISTORIC SCOTLAND
ALBA AOSMHOR

Cadw

Llywodraeth Cymru
Welsh Government

PHYSICAL LEGACY OF
THE HOME FRONT
1914–18

FIRST WORLD WAR
CENTENARY
LED BY IWM

Council for British Archaeology

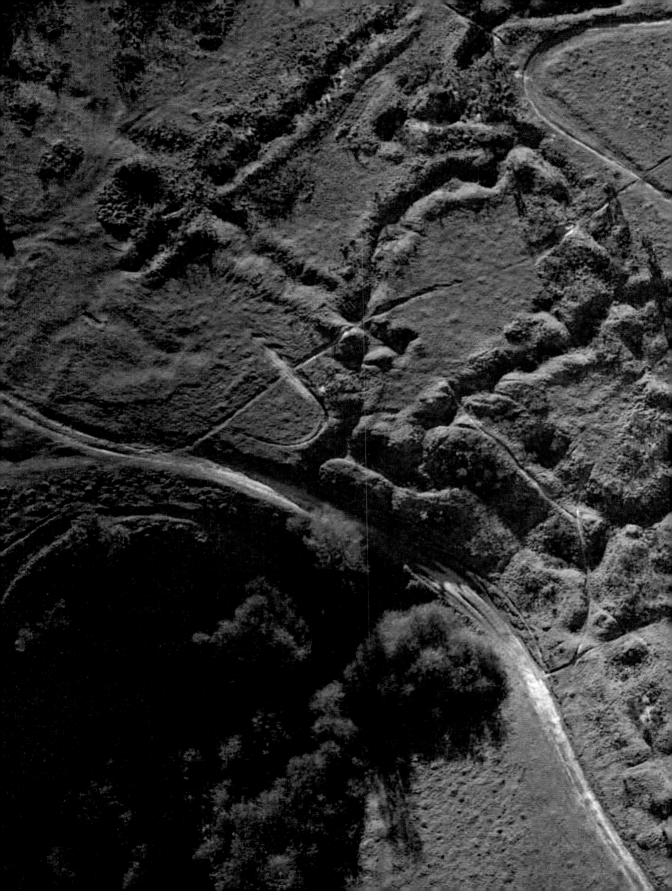

THE HOME FRONT IN
BRITAIN 1914–18:
AN ARCHAEOLOGICAL
HANDBOOK

Edited by Catrina Appleby, Wayne Cocroft
and John Schofield

CBA Practical Handbook No 22
Council for British Archaeology 2015

Published in 2015 by the Council for British Archaeology
Beatrice de Cardi House, 66 Bootham, York YO30 7BZ

British Library cataloguing in Publication Data
A catalogue record for this book is available from the British Library
ISBN 978-1-909990-01-2

DOI: 10.11141/PH22

Typeset by Carnegie Book Production
Printed and bound by Berforts Information Press, Oxford

The publisher acknowledges with gratitude generous grants from Historic
England, Historic Scotland and Cadw towards the cost of publication

Front cover: First World War practice trenches at Rothbury, Northumberland
(© English Heritage)
Back cover: U-boat entering Harwich dock (courtesy of Wayne Cocroft);
Remains of ablutions block at Cannock Chase Training Camp (© Wayne
Cocroft); War memorial, Westfield, Lancaster (© Ivan Frontani)

Contents

List of figures

List of contributors

Julie Anderson — Reader, School of History, University of Kent
Catrina Appleby — Publications Officer, Council for British Archaeology
Geoff Appleby — Retired railway manager, York
Jonathan Berry — Senior Inspector of Ancient Monuments and Archaeology, Cadw
Martin Brown — Principal Archaeologist, WYG
Paul Brown — Maritime Heritage writer and researcher
Elizabeth Bruton — Visiting Fellow, Bodleian Library, University of Oxford
Ian Buxton — Visiting Professor, School of Marine Science and Technology, University of Newcastle
Helen Caffrey — Associate Lecturer, Open University
Katie Carmichael — Investigator, Historic England
Wayne Cocroft — Senior Investigator, Historic England
Mark Dunkley — Maritime Designation Adviser, Historic England
Jonathan Finch — Senior Lecturer, Dept of Archaeology, University of York
Wendy Freer — Retired History lecturer, University of Nottingham and WEA
Allan Kilpatrick — Archaeological Investigator, Royal Commission on the Ancient and Historical Monuments of Scotland
Jeremy Lake — Historic Environment Intelligence (Landscape and Resources), Historic England
Heather Montgomery — School of Geography, Archaeology and Palaeoecology, Queen's University Belfast
Frances Moreton — Director, War Memorials Trust
Bridy Parsons — Postgraduate student
Cyril Pearce — Honorary Research Fellow, School of History, University of Leeds
John Schofield — Head of Dept, Dept of Archaeology, University of York
Paul Stamper — Senior Adviser, Historic England
Geoffrey Stell — Visiting Lecturer, Edinburgh College of Art, University of Edinburgh
Roger J C Thomas — Assistant Designation Adviser, Historic England
Jonathan Trigg — Lecturer, University of Liverpool
Sarah Tunnicliffe — National Rural and Environmental Adviser, Historic England

THE HOME FRONT IN BRITAIN 1914—18

Acknowledgements

This handbook has been written to support the Council for British Archaeology's (CBA) *Home Front Legacy 1914–18* project, details of which may be found on the CBA's website. It builds on an early handbook – *20th century defences in Britain* – published by the CBA in 1996 (Lowry ed) to assist the Heritage Lottery-funded *Defence of Britain* project. This book describes First World War remains in more detail and specifically places more emphasis on researching the impact of the war on the civilian Home Front.

This book has been compiled from contributions by many specialists in particular aspects of First World War research. The editors would like to thank the authors for their contributions and the collaborative spirit in which they were produced. The following are acknowledged as the lead authors for particular sections of the book: Julie Anderson, hospitals; Geoff Appleby, railways; Martin Brown, excavating First World War artefacts and practice trenches; Paul Brown and Ian Buxton, shipyards and naval bases; Elizabeth Bruton, wireless stations and intelligence; Helen Caffrey, Homes fit for Heroes, affordable housing, and welfare buildings and farms; Katie Carmichael, drill halls; Wayne Cocroft, introduction to the Home Front, munitions manufacture, balloon sites, anti-aircraft gun sites, and bombing; Mark Dunkley, ship and submarine wrecks; Jonathan Finch, camps; Wendy Freer, inland waterways; Jeremy Lake, introduction to air and airfields; Frances Moreton, war memorials and cemeteries; Bridy Parsons, horses; Cyril Pearce, dissent and conscientious objection; John Schofield, introduction; Paul Stamper, agriculture and Afterword; Geoffrey Stell, Scapa Flow; Roger J C Thomas, introductions to military land use and sea, and anti-invasion defence works and coastal defences; Jonathan Trigg, commemoration; Sarah Tunnicliffe, village halls. Heather Montgomery contributed notes on sites in Ireland, Allan Kilpatrick on sites in Scotland, and Jonathan Berry on sites in Wales. The editors are also grateful to Judith English and Jenny Newell, Surrey Archaeological Society, for sharing their research on Felday prisoner of war camp, and to Gordon Barclay for commenting on an early draft. Dan Snow, President of the CBA, kindly contributed the Foreword.

In particular the editors acknowledge the debt that this book owes to a pilot study funded by English Heritage and undertaken by Nicholas Saunders and Emily Glass (University of Bistol) and John Schofield (University of York). Short sections of this Introduction, and some of the examples given, originate in the project's Pilot Handbook. At the CBA we thank Mike Heyworth for his continuing encouragement and support, and Louise Ennis who developed the Home Front Legacy project. Catrina Appleby managed the publication project and provided expert editorial input.

Editors' Notes

In this book, the term 'United Kingdom' is used in its pre-1922 meaning of Britain and Ireland.

The term 'Britain' is used, as it would have been at the time, to encompass the whole of the United Kingdom.

On 1 April 2015 English Heritage split into two organisations: Historic England and the English Heritage Trust. Information on archive reports and images is now available via the Historic England website: www.historicengland.org.uk.

Foreword

The First World War gave our world order a mighty blow from which it is yet to recover. The history of the last hundred years has been shaped and coloured by the upheavals of those tragic years of war. The chaos in the Middle East, the uncertainties and conflict of Eastern Europe, the tumultuous journey of modern China, the collapse of European empires and growth of American power all owe so much to the long shadow of the First World War. I have visited the war's battlefields from the Western Front in France and Belgium to the terrifying summits of the Dolomites in Italy, from the shores of Lake Tanganyika in Tanzania to the battlefields of the Arab Revolt against Ottoman Turkish rule. They are, without exception, fascinating places to visit. On the ground you get a real sense of why events developed the way they did, and they are the perfect place to think about the seismic changes that resulted from the actions of the men and women who fought, struggled and suffered in those diverse locations. What this Handbook does so well is remind us that the legacy of the war is just as tangible here in the UK. There were no land battles here but war had a massive impact on the British people and landscape. There was violence, an aerial assault, naval bombardments, and an insurrection in Dublin, not to mention costly industrial accidents and deprivation caused by submarine blockade. I have visited the towns in north-east England which were shelled by the German navy, resulting in the first civilian losses in the UK from foreign military action in generations. I have charted the course of German airships as they crept gracefully across eastern England on bombing missions. I have visited munitions factories in Silvertown and Gretna Green which produced millions of shells to quench the unprecedented demands of modern, industrial war. This book is a vital tool for all those of us who want to research the context of the many First World War remains that we come across. Whether you are looking for more information about coastal defences, munitions production, war memorials, practice trenches that still criss-cross the landscape in many parts of the country or simply family pictures, letters and mementoes, this book will provide a wealth of detail that will hugely enrich your exploration of the First World War's physical legacy. Enjoy using this book, it will unlock a million stories of normal people, places and buildings, each one better than any made-up story.

Dan Snow
President
Council for British Archaeology

CHAPTER I

The archaeology of the Home Front

1.1   Introduction

For most people, the First World War needs no introduction. Whichever generation one belongs to, excepting perhaps the very young, there is close familiarity. Even its dates, 1914–18, resonate with historic significance and of a carnage inflicted on millions, while the place names ('The Western Front', 'Passchendaele', 'Gallipoli') are forever associated with the heat of battle, and the loss of many thousands of men. Even the words of war are deeply ingrained in our everyday language: we still speak of 'going over the top'; 'lousy' and 'crummy' refer to lice infestations, while a 'snapshot' stems from a quickly aimed and taken rifle shot. Some words emerged from the Middle Eastern campaign, such as 'cushy' from *Khush* (pleasure), and yet others from the trenches opposite: 'strafe' became an English word, from the German, 'to punish', via the slogan '*Gott Strafe England*'. Songs were penned about the war, poetry written, and a plethora of historic and contemporary literature has subsequently emerged, contributing to a national heritage redolent with deeply felt and affective legacies, although even in the 1920s, a mythology of the war was developing – 'meaningless sacrifice', 'lions led by donkeys' – that has obscured the realities. In many ways this together represents a distant world, of Empire and heavy industry, a world in which many people worked the land and lived in rural communities, while others had been swept into an industrial revolution, labouring not in fields but in factories and down mines, or building ships. Little did they know, prior to 1914, how important these products and processes were shortly to become, in feeding the industry of a calamitous and hungry war.

Visiting northern France or Belgium today, one sees a landscape, both urban and rural, that has recovered remarkably well, but the scars of this conflict are still present: every view it seems takes in a memorial or a cemetery; and small museums appear to be increasingly common with the passage of time. Yet this is not an unchanging landscape. Recent developments in the region's infrastructure have carved transects across it – high-speed railway lines and motorways. Increasingly, as a result of these incursions, archaeologists encounter the war, through the discovery of bunkers, tunnels, trench systems and burials of the fallen (Fig 1.1). Examples are well-documented and always attract media attention, not least as soldiers previously missing in action are finally identified and laid to rest with due ceremony. In the Middle East archaeologists are encountering one of the icons of the age, Lawrence of Arabia. Field work in Jordan has documented contemporary railway lines and encampments. Even in the Alps, in the mountains, the Front Line can be traced, with contemporary remains (including human remains) emerging as the glaciers melt and retreat. The scale of this legacy is almost beyond comprehension, a century on. Looking up at the Menin Gate at Ypres, or the Thiepval Memorial, and scanning the names, it is hard even to imagine so many people alive in this landscape, living, breathing, fighting, and surviving, the chaos of a slow and mechanical war. The scale only really becomes apparent when one visits the Western Front. A few years ago, a party of forty heritage professionals, on a visit to the battlefields, was each given an envelope with their name on. Within this envelope was the story of a soldier bearing their exact name (initials and surname in the case of female members of the party).

Figure 1.1 Excavation of a mass grave at Pheasant Wood, Fromelles, France in 2009; the bodies were later reburied in a new CWGC cemetery (© Oxford Archaeology)

In every case the namesake had died, and in most cases the names were to be seen on the above-named memorials. The envelopes were presented on the first morning of a four-day workshop; the message conveyed to the group remained with them throughout the visit.

Much has been made of the battlefields over the past one hundred years. Even during but especially after the conflict there was a period of mourning, not merely for the fallen but for the scarred landscape which seemed metaphorical of this great loss. In time the landscape recovered, helped by huge state investment in reconstruction, and people came to see it, as mourners and as tourists. For those with loved ones dead or missing, the landscape provided a direct and tangible connection to the husbands, sons and lovers whom they had lost (Fig 1.2). Slowly the land became productive once more, bearing crops – although even today the legacy remains, as unexploded shells are inadvertently set off, adding innocent victims to the list of casualties. After 1918 the bomb-damaged towns and villages were cleared and often then rebuilt. The great Cloth Hall at Ypres was reconstructed exactly to its original design, a classic 'phoenix', rising from the literal ashes. In the period after the Second World War, tourism (and in particular cultural tourism) became fashionable, as did genealogy as a leisure pursuit. Once again visitors flocked to the battlefields, to mourn and to learn. The inclusion of the First World War on national curricula ensured its popularity amongst school groups, to the extent that large groups of children are now a common sight at battlefield memorials, often recalling the comment of philosopher Paul Virilio, 'playful warring after the real warring'.

Useful though such visits may be in understanding the scale of the conflict on the Western Front, it is not *necessary* to travel abroad to encounter the First World War, since direct evidence can be found here in the UK. The battlefields may have been in France, Belgium, Mesopotamia, the Alps and elsewhere, but training and preparations took place at home, in training areas and factories across the country, in drill halls and farmers' fields, and in 'practice' trenches.

Figure 1.2 An early private grave, erected by the family in France. It was later replaced by a standard Imperial War Graves Commission headstone (Courtesy of Gordon Hall)

Further, with so many men away, the women at home found a new role in leading the production of war *matériel* such as shells and munitions (Fig 1.3). It is important not to underestimate the numbers involved in war work: the cordite factory at Gretna employed some 19,000 people, of which approximately two-thirds were women, and this picture was repeated across the country. It was a new role that had hidden and unexpected consequences: women from this time often sported more 'masculine' hairstyles, and smoked openly, in public. Women would never be the same again. The First World War therefore also contributed towards a social revolution.

This social impact is one thing, but there was also a strong physical impact on the landscape of the 'Home Front'. While not as pronounced perhaps as the changes to the landscape across the Channel, changes were nonetheless clearly in evidence, and these changes have influenced what survives today. There was fear of attack and invasion by Germany's armed forces, so defences were placed both along the coastline and inland, as for instance at Edinburgh Castle. Coastal erosion has put paid to many of these early defences (and also many of the Second World War) but some survive. There are places where the new recruits trained and prepared for what was to follow – training areas, drill halls and scale models like that in Staffordshire of the Messines Ridge, used to discuss and describe tactics and strategy. But most visible of all are the memorials. In every town and village, almost without exception, are the war memorials to the fallen (Fig 1.4). Every soldier named has a story, a name and two places with which they will be forever associated: the place they lived, and the place they died. Much historical and archaeological work has, unsurprisingly, focused on the places where most of these soldiers died. This Handbook focuses instead on the places where

Figure 1.3 Women workers pull trolleys of shells at the National Shell Factory, Parkgate, Dublin (© IWM)

Figure 1.4 The Cross of Sacrifice, seen here at Cannock Chase War Cemetery, was designed by Sir Reginald Blomfield and was used as a template for memorials across the country (© Wayne Cocroft)

they lived, on what happened on the Home Front as battle raged on the 'Green Fields of France', and on what survives today.

This Introduction provides the context for the details that follow. Many types of activity associated with the First World War have left a trace and our historic environment is rich with buildings, structures and earthworks, not to mention sites and places, which closely associate with a memory or a story from this period. The aim of this Handbook is to provide the information necessary to allow people of all ages and backgrounds to begin to read and understand those traces: history or archaeology from the ground up, as it were. For some, documentary sources will prove their inspiration, whilst for others trawling through media reports or local parish newsletters may provide the lead that sets hares racing. Villagers may wish to follow parish records related to a name on a local memorial. Some element of oral history might be preferred, not for those directly recalling the conflict of course, but perhaps second- or third-generation accounts, for example of children or grandchildren who recall the stories they were told, or who have mementoes handed down by parents or grandparents. Finally there is scope for archaeological research, by investigating aerial photographs or scrabbling through woodland for traces of long-lost structures or trenches, or becoming involved in community-led fieldwork or excavation projects. Others yet may wish to work with museums to catalogue and describe artefacts held in local collections. Whatever one's preferences, there is the chance to get involved. This Handbook helps by describing possibilities, and highlighting the things to look out for.

Previous encounters

Archaeology is a subject with a long history, dating back at least to the 17th century in terms of archaeological practice in Britain, although it wasn't until the late 19th century that it started to develop into the discipline we see today. Heritage protection also emerged at this time, with the first ancient monuments legislation. However, to most people archaeology was seen as relating to the distant past, be it medieval or prehistoric, and it was not until the late 1950s that the concept of 'industrial archaeology' emerged, let alone the archaeology of 20th-century conflicts. But from the 1960s, with increased leisure time, amateur archaeology became in vogue, and cultural participation increased as a result. Many of the first participants in amateur conflict archaeology were former soldiers, sailors and airmen with an interest in the past and some of these amateur archaeological investigators tackled the topics professional archaeologists left alone. Henry Wills' national study of Second World War Pillboxes (published in 1985 but reflecting years of work) is an example, and one that paved the way for the eventual Defence of Britain project (1995–2002), a national survey funded by the Department for National Heritage (now DCMS) and the Heritage Lottery Fund which mobilised some 600 amateur and hugely enthusiastic archaeologists to generate an impressive and comprehensive record of Second World War anti-invasion defences, complementing the documentary study of other categories of Second World War and earlier sites expertly compiled for English Heritage by Colin Dobinson with additional and related studies for Wales, Scotland and Northern Ireland.

The various anniversaries relating to the Second World War in the 1990s, together with the approaching 100th anniversary of the First World War, have led to a dramatic upsurge of interest in the archaeology of recent conflict, with the UK-based national agencies commissioning research to support the inevitable increase in heritage protection applications for conflict-related sites. The Council for British Archaeology (CBA) has played a crucial role in supporting these research initiatives, and in implementing the Defence of Britain project (DoB). The CBA also produced the DoB Handbook which volunteers used to identify sites and structures, and to determine the appropriate means by which to record them. These projects have led to academic research, to the point now where recent conflicts feature prominently in some undergraduate and postgraduate archaeology programmes alongside the more conventional periods of archaeological study. Books and papers on the subject appear regularly in mainstream journals and a dedicated *Journal of Conflict Archaeology* is now firmly established. The archaeology of recent conflict has also matured into studies that cross established disciplinary boundaries and employ high standards in field survey and excavation. In summary, the subject has developed from an amateur pursuit, studied often by retired servicemen in their leisure time, to being embedded within the research agenda of leading heritage organisations and higher education institutions. Like industrial archaeology before it, conflict archaeology is now firmly established in the mainstream, to the considerable advantage of those wishing to study the First World War on the Home Front.

1.2 Sources

Embarking on a research project or individual study for the first time can be a daunting prospect, but with some simple guidelines and an impression of what to look for, the task can be rendered less intimidating and more manageable. This Handbook is framed largely as a kind of 'spotter's guide', a series of 'snapshots' which together provide an indicative overview of the resource. Such overviews can never be definitive, partly in view of the subtle and often regional variations in design of buildings, for example, and partly due to the scale of the resource. We also do not know what, precisely, is out there, which is of course where you come in! This section will not pre-empt the descriptions and analyses that make up this *Handbook*, but it can outline some of the sources one might usefully consult as a starting point. The assumption here is that most readers and researchers will be focused on a particular place or area, as opposed to taking a broader, thematic approach. These broader studies are often undertaken by larger organisations and agencies and tend to work best when they synthesise locally held data. Thus work by individuals and groups as part of the Home Front Legacy Project can make a valuable contribution to our overall understanding of the period through data gathering.

Carrying out research today is a rather different experience from what it was even ten years ago: the rise of the internet has made it possible to retrieve a huge mass of data on almost anything without even leaving home. Some will be irrelevant, some poorly constructed, and some may be inaccurate, but one can almost always find at least a few nuggets of useful information. The internet is an opportunity as well as a resource, allowing one to share information as well as acquire it.

Historic Environment Records

We should begin with the Historic Environment Records, or HERs. These were previously known as Sites and Monument Records or SMRs, but the name changed as their role and scope extended from only sites and monuments (places) to encompass buildings and the wider landscape. Every local authority within the UK has a Historic Environment Record of some kind, typically comprising many thousands of individual records for sites and monuments, historic buildings, places where artefacts have been found, features (such as ancient fields) visible not on the ground surface but on aerial photographs, place names that hint at some former use of which no material trace survives, and so on. Some of these records can only be consulted by visiting the local authority offices (often the HER is held within the Planning Department), for which a prior appointment should be made, but increasingly, these records are available and accessible, freely, online; it is worth checking. One can easily do this by using the 'Heritage Gateway' website or by inserting key words into a search engine: 'Norfolk' and 'Historic Environment Record', for example, or by searching within a local authority website. In Wales, the HERs maintained by the Archaeological Trusts can be consulted online using the *Archwilio* service. A basic search can usually be conducted without the need to register, but registration will typically open up additional opportunities, and reveal further information. Registration is also helpful for the local authority: these essential services are often threatened when local authority budgets are cut, and data on the numbers of users and the nature of their enquiries may help to justify their existence. Search facilities within the HERs vary but will usually include the option to search by geographical area (eg parish) or by period, or by site type, and any combination of these. Once sites are identified the information

can typically include a short description, any further (eg published) sources, plans or photographs, and even in some cases aerial photographs. Often though the 'online' record is only an indication of what more can be found within the actual (physical) HER, which can be consulted by making an appointment. The physical HER will also often contain a series of early (eg Ordnance Survey) maps on which one might see buildings that no longer survive, meaning one can then pinpoint the location in advance of a site visit.

HERs then are a particularly useful, and typically (and increasingly) accessible, record, but they are merely a record of what is currently known. The wonderful thing about archaeology is the sense that there is so much more to discover, places and things that are not yet known or often even imagined. The HER therefore is only a starting point. It tells you about the 'known knowns', in Donald Rumsfeld's terms, and to some extent the 'known unknowns' (sites known about but currently unlocated on the ground). While you can help with both of these, by providing further information, and enhancing the record, you can also 'go for the gaps' (the 'unknown unknowns', where new discoveries come as a genuine surprise)! HER staff will not be upset or offended if you find new things, or find errors or shortcomings in their data. Any record is only as good as the data it contains, and if through your endeavours you are able to supplement or update the record, this will be welcomed.

In all parts of the UK the national heritage agencies maintain archaeological records which are easily accessible online: in England the *PastScape* website; in Scotland, *Canmore*; in Wales, *Coflein*; and in Northern Ireland, the NI Sites and Monuments Record. In Scotland and England, the national and

Figure 1.5 Workers' huts at the National Factory, Gretna: an example of an aerial photograph from the Aerofilms Archive. These images are now available via the *Britain from Above* website (© RCAHMS)

many local HERs can be accessed through the Pastmap and Heritage Gateway websites respectively, and similarly in Wales through the *Historic Wales* website. These national archives also hold plans, photographs, and thousands of aerial photographs, collected and collated over a long period, and comprising both vertical and oblique images covering much of the country. An important collection of early aerial photographs by the *Aerofilms* company has recently been made accessible online on the *Britain from Above* website (Fig 1.5). Many of the photographs taken during the 1920s offer a unique record of Britain's First World War landscape. While there will be some repetition and overlap (and perhaps even some contradictions) between these 'national' records and the 'locally held' HERs, they are significant and are worth consulting, again online in the first instance. As with HERs, having established what may exist within these online records, consulting the physical record may be worthwhile.

The National Archives

The National Archives (at Kew, London) is a public archive of documentary records held, for example, by government departments. A previous national study of these archives, as they pertain to sites built for defence during the Second World War, demonstrated how complete and comprehensive these records can be for some areas. This project, carried out by Colin Dobinson and Neil Redfern and funded by the national heritage agencies (*c* 1995–2002), examined what was built where, when and why (eg anti-aircraft artillery, coastal artillery, bombing decoys, etc). In England these documented sites were then examined on contemporary aerial photographs to determine modern survival (or not, in most cases) leading to informed recommendations for statutory protection, on the grounds that these rare survivals were of 'national importance'. Although focused primarily on the Second World War, the study confirmed the survival of some records for First World War sites. While one must visit The National Archives to consult most of the actual records (although more and more is now available digitally), online searches can be undertaken in advance, saving time on the day.

Record Offices and Museums

On a more local scale, local authority archives (not to be confused with HERs, but typically also managed and maintained by the local authority) can be a rich source of information. In addition to early editions of local maps, these offices also hold local newspapers and parish magazines, containing stories about people and places at this time. Once names and/or places have been identified, one can then use additional sources such as trade listings (eg Kelly's Post Office Directories) to research people's associations with particular buildings. It should be added that, with the upsurge of popular interest in the First World War, many local archives have followed the example of national bodies like The National Archives in providing excellent and specific 'Research the First World War' type Guidance Notes and 'self-help' booklets and webpages. The Imperial War

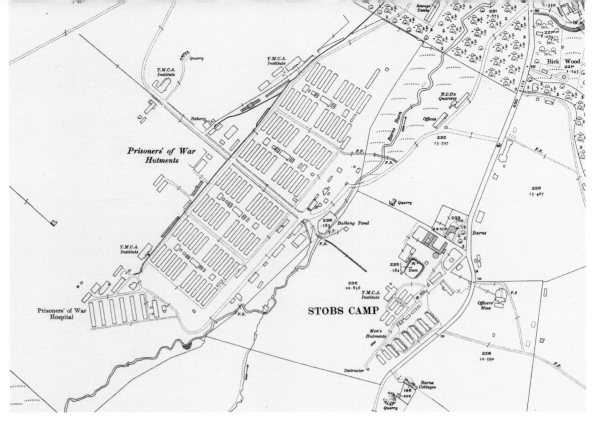

Figure 1.6 The large military training camp at Stobs, in the Scottish Borders, as depicted on the OS map of 1920. The site also housed a large PoW camp (Reproduced by permission of the National Library of Scotland)

Museum holds a vast amount of materal relating to the Home Front, including artefacts, films, photographs, books, documents and oral history recordings. Many may be viewed in their online catalogue, while other material will need to viewed in person in London. In Wales, a variety of primary sources relating to the First World War from the libraries, special collections and archives of Wales have been digitised. Regimental and service museums also maintain important collections of records and pictures relating to local regiments and volunteer units. They may also hold information about other camps where a regiment was stationed. For some units, such as the Royal Engineers and Royal Artillery, there are single national museums. Similarly, the Royal Navy Museum at Portsmouth, the Royal Naval Air Service Museum at Yeovilton, the Royal Air Force Museum at Hendon, and the National Army Museum, Chelsea, all possess collections relating to their interests.

Maps, in particular Ordnance Survey maps, are integral within all of the sources listed above, but have value in their own right as key sources of information for this period. Examination of those published before the war can help in the identification of features such as drill halls or firing ranges of the Territorial Army, while those published soon after may record airfields and munitions factories, as well as military and prisoner of war camps, such as that at Stobs, near Hawick in Scotland (Fig 1.6), although if a site remained active into the inter-war period it may not be depicted. Many files in The National Archives also contain maps: some are catalogued as separate items, while others may only be found by a personal visit. In other instances local record offices may hold plans from post-war auction sales.

Researching munitions factories

During the war, hundreds of factories were set up across the country to manufacture explosives, shells, and all types of war *matériel*. The variety and quality of surviving documents relating to individual munitions factories will vary greatly and there are potentially many sources of information. At a national level administrative files may survive at The National Archives, Kew, and in some instances these contain pictures of the factories, often while being constructed. By the early 1920s many of the factories had been sold and were mapped on 1 to 25 inch Ordnance Survey maps, which are generally available in local record offices. These may provide a detailed plan of a works, but will rarely identify buildings by function. The *Aerofilms* collection of aerial photographs often shows industrial areas with wartime factories either still in use, or shortly after closure. The many photographs of munitions factories taken during the four years of the war represent one of the most intensive records of industry and working life ever produced. This vast legacy yields valuable information on working conditions, the roles and activities undertaken by men and women, their ages, clothing, machinery and plant – things which rarely survive as historical artefacts (Fig 1.7). Some images are readily accessible through the Imperial War Museum's website, and others may survive in local record offices and private collections. Company histories should also be consulted as many will proudly tell of their role in the Great War.

Figure 1.7 Practice shot and shrapnel shells in bay 4 of No 1 Machine Shop at the National Projectile Munitions Factory, Hall Street, Dudley (Reproduced by permission of English Heritage)

1.3 Artefacts and mementoes

Much of this chapter, and the book, is about places where vestiges of the First World War survive on the Home Front, in the form of earthwork trenches, buildings and memorials. Much also survives in local and national archives. But what is frequently forgotten is the potential to find a mass of information in museum stores and private collections, or in people's cupboards and lofts, in the form of artefacts, objects and mementoes. These artefacts are often precious items, rare survivals of once common objects, and which each tell a story. Often the people to whom that story was once told are able to retell it to younger generations, but in many cases, without the artefact surviving as a prompt, an *aide memoire*, the stories are frequently forgotten. Equally the artefacts may outlive those able to tell their story. In this section some of the main types of artefacts are described, and cross-referenced to the types of places most commonly associated with them.

The British 'Tommy' carried an array of equipment that varied by role, mission or activity. Each man was defined by his cap badge and the brass shoulder titles with the name of his regiment or specialist corps. In addition to uniform and boots he would also wear a set of either 1914-pattern leather, or 1908-pattern thick cotton, webbing (Fig 1.8) onto which he was able to attach two sizes of knapsack, bayonet, entrenching tool and water bottle, as well as 150 rounds (bullets) of .303 rifle ammunition. Fully laden he might carry as much as 70lb (32kg) of kit, while following the first use of chemical weapons by the Germans in 1915 all men were also issued with a gas mask or respirator. By 1916 all men also carried the Brodie steel helmet (a 'tin hat'). All of this could be supplemented by spades, flashlights, wire cutters, army biscuits and tinned food, and any number of other military accoutrements, as well as personal effects. Each man carried his own mess tins, clasp knife, shaving kit and two cloth rolls. The larger was the Holdall, which included a variety of useful objects such as comb, toothbrush and knife, fork and spoon, as well as the Button Stick, a piece of brass with a slot that allowed brass buttons to be polished without the polish staining the uniform. The utensils were usually stamped with the Service number of the owner and toothbrush handles may also be inscribed because such objects were not things men were keen on sharing! The smaller 'Hussif' (Housewife) contained sewing materials and spare buttons, allowing the uniform to be kept in good order. Perishable materials carried included the Pay Book, Bibles, which were distributed by both the army and religious bodies, and, for Officers, the 'Field Service Pocket Book'. Unfortunately, also made of perishable, compressed fibreboard were the two Identity Discs worn by all ranks, meaning that few will survive, at least in the field. The issue of equipment and clothing was a serious matter and regular kit inspections were made. Any loss or damage could result in sanction ('Being on a Charge') leading to fatigues (extra work) or more formal Field Punishment. While the rigours of active service might result in damage to, or loss of artefacts, from buttons upwards, life in Britain was less likely to see casual loss and proximity to stores meant losses could be made up. That said, ammunition was expended in vast

Figure 1.8 A British soldier with 1908 webbing (Courtesy of Wayne Cocroft)

quantities in training. Grenade fragments and cartridge cases will afford information to the use of parts of the training landscape but may carry other data. British cartridges were all marked with the date and place of their manufacture (although many were old, and thus can be misleading) and .303 calibre ammunition was sourced from India and the Americas, as well as British manufacturies (K for Kynoch of Birmingham being the most common). Different calibres will also indicate different weapon types employed.

Nevertheless, the British Tommy was not always marching in full kit and laden like a Christmas Tree. Soldiers would go relatively lightly equipped for their two- to four-day 'turn' in the trenches, leaving much of their personal equipment behind the lines, and when in training or on home service, webbing was not always worn, either in camp or when 'walking out' in the surrounding area. For many troops the swagger stick was a popular personal purchase. These are often shown in photographs taken in or near training camps and were made of wood or bamboo cane with a finial and, sometimes, a ferrule. The best examples had a metal finial that might show the regimental insignia, while other, cheaper examples had plain finials. These pieces were allegedly popular with officers because they stopped men walking round with their hands in their pockets! Men might also carry musical instruments, such as the concertinas shown on a photo from Cannock Chase, or the harmonicas found at St Yvon in Belgium and at Serre, where one was found amongst the effects of its owner Unteroffizier Alber Thielecke. Troops were often entertained a short distance behind the lines by their own regimental brass or pipe bands. Free time also afforded an opportunity for writing and sketching and drawing materials and watercolours might be carried. In addition, as smoking was a commonplace activity, smoking paraphernalia is frequently found, including pipes and cigarette tins. Other effects may be utterly mundane, such as the lid of a jar, a railway ticket, a watch or loose change, while some may be more unusual, such as a prehistoric flint scraper, perhaps picked up out of curiosity or interest.

Religion and ritual were an important part of life. The army had a Chaplaincy, which provided succour to troops and organised religious services (mainly Christian but other religions were also provided for). In camps there were chapels of various denominations in huts and men carried religious paraphernalia, including rosaries amongst Roman Catholics. Ritual practice carried into uniform from the civilian world was also approved of by the military authorities as a way of strengthening bonds between men, and this was manifest in material culture including Masonic artefacts or the pipe associated with the rituals of the Royal Antediluvian Order of Buffalos found at Brocton Camp, Staffordshire. Individual charms have also been identified, including trench art talismans made from bullets or touchstones, such as the ivory or resin monkey found with its owner at Fromelles and perhaps the flint scraper referred to above. While these charms seem to embody some personal attachment other lucky charms, such as the 'Touch Wood', were mass produced. Unusual ritual practice may also be demonstrated by the empty champagne bottles and smashed dinner service found during excavation of a dugout on training grounds at Colchester. This may reflect a Mess Night, one of the bonding rituals for army officers.

The mobilisation of a large part of the male population, and the attendant massive expansion of the military, required the supply of a significant volume of everyday objects to support military training and operations. Army camps drew on the Staffordshire potteries for instance to provide the plain white plates and bowls used by each man in barracks. Meanwhile support services, including the YMCA and Church Army, also needed to equip their institutes as places where men could go during periods of relaxation. Amongst ceramic assemblages some material will be marked with the Board of Ordnance broad arrow or 'Crow Foot', or the War Department 'W' within a lozenge, but others may carry identification of their owners, such as the Navy and Army Catering Board, whose ceramic is marked NACB. Material clearly associated with individual units is less common, though one fragment decorated with the Machine-gun Corps crest and the words 'A Service Battn' was found during works at Belton Camp. Further common finds have been fragments of 'pleasant strawberry-pink china' beer mugs of the type referred to by George Orwell in his description of the perfect pub, *The Moon Under Water*. These are unlikely to be associated with alcohol within the bounds of the camp and may have been requisitioned for non-alcoholic beverages, the colour discouraging pilfering by soldiers! In addition to ceramics associated with food and drink, large numbers of ink bottles have been identified on sites including Cannock Chase and Belton. These objects embody the massive bureaucracy necessary to raise, train, supply, feed and deploy military forces.

Glass has been found to make up a significant part of the assemblages found at camps. The range of jars and bottles is indicative of life within any camp and, to an extent, at the Front. Beer and wine bottles may be indicative of official or covert consumption but may equally have been used for water supply. Bovril and Camp Coffee bottles indicate the quantities of these concentrated beverages consumed and are indicative of the power of a hot drink to restore morale. Brown sauce bottles, including both HP and OK Sauce brands, and jars for pickles clearly demonstrate the repetitive and, to some tastes, bland nature of army catering – something the modern army acknowledges by the inclusion of Tabasco in ration packs. Medicine bottles may reflect the effect of gathering men together from around the nation, packing them into barracks, and subjecting them to physical, outdoor activity in all weathers. They also reflect the fact that some camps, such as Brocton, Staffordshire, Bovington, Dorset, and Bron Aber at Transfynydd, Gwynedd had their 'tin towns' akin to the *vici* that developed at the gates of Roman forts to provide goods and services to the soldiers. Tellingly, Eno's Fruit Salts bottles may reflect poor food, or a delicate soldier's constitution. Off-duty activity may also be evident in objects such as an Anzora bottle. This hair tonic was a precursor to Brylcreem and more modern hair gels and its presence on a camp site may reflect the recruits' intention to go into town looking for fun. Evidence of the global nature of the conflict may also be seen in the items found: Tavu boot polish was brought to Britain by New Zealanders and its bottles have been found at the New Zealand Rifle Brigade camp at Brocton.

At the Front, food tins are common discoveries, but the picture is very different within the United Kingdom. While tins for corned beef – the ubiquitous Front Line 'Bully Beef' – or stew are frequent finds on the former battlefields, they are scarce in Britain. Fresh food could easily be provided for troops safe at home, whereas the supply and storage of supplies for the trenches was more complicated, making tinned food vital to the maintenance of the Front. However, tins for petrol, water, oil, foot powder and polish for both boots and buttons may be anticipated. The famous Princess Mary tins given to all those 'wearing the King's uniform on Christmas Day 1914' contained item such as cigarettes, sweets and pencils, as well as a picture of the Princess.

It should be remembered that indigenous British forces were not the only soldiers in Britain; soldiers from the Dominions, Canada, Australia and New Zealand, as well as India were also trained and stationed here and will have left distinctive items of equipment and personal belongings, while German prisoners of war were transported to Britain and held in prison camps. Where this was the case indicative finds may be anticipated, including uniform elements, such as the German buttons found at Yatesbury, Wiltshire.

The Great War was an industrial, global conflict. The whole resources of not only the warring nations, but also neutral states supplying the combatants were geared to war production, whether directly, through *matériel* or in production of the foodstuffs, medicines, crockery and 'the things they carried'. Once peace came, most of the temporary towns of the training and transit camps were swiftly dismantled. During this work much was sold, lost, or broken and discarded. Nevertheless, the debris left by the camps' occupants may still be identified in clearance and demolition middens, or scattered around hut sites and within barrack footprints where objects had fallen through the floorboards. Not only can these objects provide an insight into the military experience, but the location of particular finds, such as pink mugs, ammunition or ink wells may provide useful information for understanding parts of the camp, in the same way artefacts would be used to aid investigations of more traditional archaeological sites. Artefacts from First World War sites, the utilitarian, personal, military and civilian, all embody the experience of the population during the Great War, whether recruited man, factory worker, loved one sending a gift, or manufacturer and shop keeper responding to new markets.

1.4 Sites and places

One of the principal purposes of this Handbook is to describe the types of sites and structures one might expect to find from this period on the Home Front. It may be helpful, at this point, to highlight the two axes within which one might approach this. One is to work geographically, in a particular area (typically a parish, a town, a region (such as a valley), a district or 'county') or thematically; both have their advantages. Working geographically allows one to build a picture of the impact of military activity within an area over time. One might think of a military training area, for example, which as well as traces of activity from the First and Second World Wars, may also have evidence of preparations for earlier 19th-century conflict and the later Cold War. In such situations all the remains should be recorded, as this is primarily a story of continuity. The challenge often is to work out the phasing of such sites. Thematic studies, on the other hand, allow the researcher to build a detailed view of a particular type of site, and understand it in strategic and geographical terms. Coastal defence of an area thought particularly vulnerable to seaborne invasion could be one example, although in some cases earlier and later evidence for coastal defence may also survive.

To remain with the thematic approach, the main categories of site provide a useful framework within which to identify a subject for research. One might think in terms of 'civilian, domestic and agricultural' sites for example, or industrial sites. One might rather focus on the discrete and clearly defined subject of military defence and training, or memorials. Or one might think about hospitals and convalescent care.

The scope is vast under 'civilian, domestic and agriculture'. One might envisage for example studies of agricultural and forestry landscapes which saw increased food and timber production to serve the 'war effort'. Spaces such as school playing fields and village greens were used as vegetable plots, and some of these survive today as allotments; these sites may have been associated with the Women's Land Army. Air-raid shelters and first-aid posts were created through the construction and modification of buildings, while other buildings (often people's houses) were used for Civil Defence planning, Red Cross meetings or for knitting or bandage rolling. The former role of some buildings may survive in records or as second-hand memories, even though the fabric of the building may show no trace of these ephemeral activities. The same may be true of places which hosted fund-raising rallies and concerts, or served as salvage collection depots. One example is that of Grove House in King Street, Ashton-under-Lyne, registered as a Hospital Supply Depot in 1915. Such places were used for creating roller and triangular bandages, swabs and dressings. Country estates were requisitioned for camps and training, or for organisational reasons. There are also places where specific events occurred, or where notable people associated with the First World War lived or worked.

The First World War was the first large-scale industrial war, and it is no surprise therefore that wartime industrial buildings are heavily inscribed on

THESE PREMISES
WERE TOTALLY DESTROYED
BY A
ZEPPELIN RAID
DURING THE WORLD WAR
ON
SEPTEMBER 8TH 1915
REBUILT 1917

JOHN PHILLIPS
GOVERNING DIRECTOR

Figure 1.9 A plaque recording a Zeppelin attack in London (© Jerry Young)

the early 20th-century landscape. While many such buildings have been lost, much nonetheless survives. In fact an example of research which combines the thematic and the regional approaches outlined above has demonstrated the significance of industry within the Lea Valley in Hertfordshire. Jim Lewis's work has shown that, in addition to well-known industrial complexes such as the Enfield Royal Small Arms Factory, Middlesex, a wide range of industries existed here, a fact illustrated through archival sources and physical survival. Within this category one might expect to see examples of industrial structures and associated new settlements. One will encounter factories related to chemical, ammunition and gas industries as well as communication technologies and associated welfare facilities. There will also be examples of weapons, military equipment and machinery factories, including some which had been adapted from a pre-war focus on items that bore no relation to the war effort.

Military defence and training is perhaps the area of study that first springs to mind with a project such as this and will appeal to many researchers. These are the places and areas across the rural and urban landscapes which fulfilled the essential purpose of military organisation, training and mobilisation. It is a diverse theme: examples might include buildings used for command and administration as well as camps and training areas. Military airfields marked a departure from previous conflicts, with the recent developments in flying. Coastal and air defence sites were created to defend against possible coastal or airborne attack or to repel invasion attempts, these typically including barrage balloon sites, guns and searchlight positions. Transportation was essential to the infrastructure, in providing supply and distribution lines. Men 'signed up' at specific locations, while march routes and departure points marked clear 'staging posts' along the way. The military communications networks were key, as were military animal collection and training centres. The army was also responsible for holding thousands of prisoners of war. Initially they were accommodated in tented camps, and later purpose-built camps, while others were interned in former workhouses or dispersed to smaller work camps. From a completely different perspective, places that came under attack have typically lived long in the memory – places that were attacked in Zeppelin raids, for example, and which are now often subject to some form of commemoration (Fig 1.9).

The obvious and urgent need to increase significantly the numbers of hospitals and hospital beds makes hospitals and convalescent care an important category. Numerous civilian hospitals and other large buildings were converted to military use at this time, by permission of the government or local authorities, while many auxiliary and private hospitals run by the Red Cross or the Order of St John were created in public and private buildings. The category is diverse therefore, embracing country houses and estates, government and ecclesiastical buildings requisitioned or donated for wartime use, military hospitals, temporary welfare camps for medical staff and patients, specialist hospitals for treatment and after-care of soldiers suffering from gas poisoning, mental health issues (or more prosaicly, veneral disease), for example, as well as medical facilities for refugees and prisoners of war, and places for rest and convalescence. In High Barnet, a Mr Davies converted his greengrocer's shop to a place of rest and shelter for convalescing soldiers. Like many other examples, the shop floor was redesigned as a patriotically decorated environment where recuperating soldiers could meet to play board games and cards.

In the popular imagination the First World War is characterised by the huge loss of life and devastation of the Western Front in France and Belgium. Far less well-known was the war fought immediately off Britain's shores. A couple of days after the outbreak of war the German mine-layer *Konigin Luise* was active off Harwich, but was soon intercepted and sunk by HMS *Lance*, although a day later one of her mines claimed HMS *Amphion*. This day-to-day battle of the mines continued throughout the war, with huge defensive minefields laid along the east coast to protect coastal shipping and across the Channel to safeguard the vital supply lines to the Continent, and offensive mine barriers such as that laid across the North Sea from Scotland to Norway by the US Navy working from bases in Scotland. This routine, but deadly, war was punctuated by dramatic attacks by German U-boats, most infamously in May 1915 on the *Lusitania* with the loss of over 1000 lives. A year later the nation was shocked by the loss off Orkney of HMS *Hampshire* to a mine and the drowning of her famous passenger Lord Kitchener. Evidence for this largely forgotten conflict remains on the sea bed and accounts for many known and dated ship wrecks off our coasts. The majority are the last resting places of their crews, who may be acknowledged on memorials to the missing, sometimes linking the consequences of the war at sea to places not normally associated with maritime affairs.

Many places along the coast gave vital support to the war at sea; the south Wales coalfield, for example, was to provide much of the coal for the Fleet. Dockyards, harbours and ports were all crucial to the operation and safety of merchant shipping and naval forces. Fishing fleets continued to provide much-needed food supplies and trawlers were converted to hunt for deadly catches of explosive mines. From its invention at the turn of the 20th century the world's leading navies quickly appreciated the potential of wireless communications and were instrumental in the rapid development of this new industry. Around Britain's shores existing commercial wireless stations were taken over for government use and intercept stations established to listen to German wireless messages. New airfields were also built to house airships and seaplanes engaged in escorting convoys and warning of the approach of hostile U-boats and surface raiders.

Finally, commemoration provides the majority and most publicly visible and recognised traces from this period, often being central to the annual ceremonies of remembrance and a focus of school visits and project work. But as well as the classic war memorials, the fallen, and frequently their comarades who survived, are remembered in a variety of other locations. These range from the dedicated war cemeteries and designated areas within existing cemeteries to street shrines and the rolls of honour in churches, schools, work places and even sports clubs (Fig 1.10). Nor do all such monuments date to the early 20th century: at Glasnevin Cemetery, Dublin the newly commissioned Cross of Sacrifice had its foundation stone laid in March 2014, to mark the Centenary of the First World War. This is the first such memorial in the south of Ireland.

These are just some of the categories and site types one might encounter when embarking on either thematic or geographically defined studies of the Home Front. As stated earlier, the purpose of this Handbook is to provide background detail, as a means to inform and advise researchers who may be unfamiliar with this field of study in their endeavours, using recording standards that will generate meaningful and useful records, and a common language.

Figure 1.10 The impressive memorial to the Prudential Insurance employees outside the company's former headquarters in Waterhouse Square, London (© Paul Stamper)

1.5 Recording field remains

Any field recording project has the capacity to generate large quantities of data, in the form of descriptive text, details (such as dimensions and information about the site's condition), and locational information as well as sketch maps and photographs. Records will vary in terms of the amount of detail people consider necessary or appropriate, and perceptions on such things as condition – a well-preserved site for one person might be poorly preserved for another. But two key words can help address any problems this might present: CONSISTENCY and TRANSPARENCY. Whatever standards and practices you employ, employ them consistently across your survey; and ensure that all of the decisions and judgement you make are explained, not necessarily at length but sufficient to reveal your thought processes to those who use your records in the future. In terms of interpretation, one might say: 'I believe this structure to be [X] based on its likeness to [Y] and the fact that the rooms are aligned ...' etc. Or on condition: 'In my opinion this site is poorly preserved and in need of some remedial works to stabilise it. The brickwork is crumbling ... [etc]. I think it is worth preserving in view of the fact that nothing comparable survives in this area and ...' etc.

In conducting fieldwork some things are crucial. One must have the permission of the landowner to access the land and any sites on it. If in doubt, visit local farms and properties to ask if anyone knows who owns a particular land parcel. Even if this draws a blank, what information and contacts you do make may become helpful later, for subsequent visits. If at all possible, use the Recording Form available via the website. If not, some baseline information is critical. If you have information already, from national records or the local HER, then ensure that this is referred to in your notes or site report. This is essential for cross references and will prevent anyone from thinking that two very similar sites co-exist in close proximity. You should record the Site Type; this information can be established using this Handbook, and using a standard terminology which exists as a thesaurus of site types (see Appendix 1). People will also need to know precisely *where* it is, which means using a six- or eight-figure National Grid Reference. Grid references can be established online through the following website:

http://gridreferencefinder.com/gmap.php

Postcodes can be established in a similar way, and these too are useful in accurately locating sites, particularly buildings.

You should also record what the site is made of (brick, concrete, earthwork). Also essential is the date of the survey and the names of those involved. A sketch plan is always useful, as is information on the current land use, any obvious threats to the stability of the site, and its present condition. This was referred to earlier as a potential source of inconsistency within the record, but in assessing whether the condition is Good or Poor, for example, one might usefully remember that the comparison here is not with modern equivalents, but with other sites that have survived, often unloved and untreated, for a hundred years. If a building or structure is more or less intact, and its original shape, form, extent and configuration can still be established (if, in other words, one can still

Health & Safety and Heritage Crime

This Handbook is designed to encourage the non-intrusive survey of the legacy of the First World War and much work to locate and record First World War sites may be achieved online or in local record offices. If you decide to undertake fieldwork to confirm the location and condition of sites, or to carry out more detailed surveys, consideration must be given to the health and safety of the survey team. If you are a member of a club or society they will probably hold insurance for field excursions and fieldwork. Before you start any fieldwork you will need to obtain permission to enter on to private land from the landowner/occupier, regardless of the status, or perceived status, of the land. Remember that all land has an owner. Many of the former military and industrial sites described in this book may contain unforeseen hazards and if you decide to extend your research to artefact collection or excavation considerably more planning will be required to guard against possible risks. In particular provision must be made to recover safely any munitions that might be discovered; this might, for example, include live rifle rounds dropped in practice trenches. Details of websites with H&S information can be found in the *Sources* section of this book.

If you find evidence of illicit metal detecting and digging, night hawking, or damage to protected monuments and structures this should be reported to the Police. You should call 999 when it is an emergency, such as when a crime is in progress or someone suspected of a crime is nearby. You should call 101 to report crime and other concerns that do not require an emergency response. An anonymous report may be made through Crimestoppers. A growing number of police services have officers who deal with matters relating to Heritage and Cultural Property Crime. Ask the call-handler to notify this officer of the offences you are reporting.

'read' the building or site in terms of its original or adapted purpose) then it may be in Good condition. The recently recorded First World War practice trenches at Gosport in Hampshire for example are partly infilled through natural soil movement, and very overgrown, but that is hardly surprising! What matters more is that they survive largely intact and legible within the contemporary landscape.

Many of your records will be saved on the computer. These should be filed, backed-up and stored. File names should be such that they provide information relevant to quick searching (for example if you need to retrieve a specific record for comparison), such as Suffolk_HOSPITALS_sitenamereport.doc. Illustrations and photographs would then be linked via that site name. You can arrange all of the information relating to this particular site in a sub-folder, within a folder on HOSPITALS, all within a folder for Suffolk. Good record keeping is important. It makes it very hard to navigate your records without this.

1.6 Conclusions

In spite of its comparatively recent date, the fact that for many readers of this Handbook the First World War was merely one generation removed, and that for long it has been a core part of our education and upbringing, little has been recorded of the First World War on the Home Front. The scale of this discrepancy has only become obvious in the last few years, since the archaeology of the conflict has returned to public attention in advance of the (then upcoming) centenary. Archaeologists have only very recently started looking for traces of the war here at home, and the results thus far have been surprising. The model built on Cannock Chase in Staffordshire, in preparation for the Messines Offensive in 1917 is one example, as are the aforementioned trenches in Gosport. The fact that many pillboxes previously thought to be of Second World War date are in fact much earlier, and that numerous projects are now meaningfully adding to the knowledge base by excavating camps and defences, shows how much we still have to learn. One approach is to leave this work 'to the experts'; the specialists with experience and knowledge in recording and understanding these places. However, archaeology has become the popular subject it is by *including* the public, not relegating them to the role of passive spectators. Like the Defence of Britain Project before it, this project provides an opportunity for people to engage with the remains of the First World War, here on the Home Front, creating a lasting and meaningful record for the benefit of this and future generations.

CHAPTER 2

Military preparations and training

2.1 Introduction

From the middle of the 19th century many of the innovative companies that defined the age through the spread of railway networks, steam ships, and ambitious civil engineering projects also turned their ingenuity to the production of armaments. Rapid developments in metallurgy and production methods, for example, allowed huge advances in the range of guns on land and at sea. These developments went hand-in-hand with the adoption of more energetic chemical explosives, which added both increased range and destructive power. Mass-production techniques, in part developed in military arsenals, ensured that vast citizen armies could be readily equipped.

With the growth in the power and size of armaments and of standing armies came the acquisition by states across Europe of increasingly large areas for sophisticated land and coastal defences, troop accommodation, training and testing areas. From the outbreak of the First World War all these trends accelerated and, as described elsewhere in this book, land was also needed for new munitions plants and airfields.

Examples of modern military training fieldworks are known from the 18th century and during the Victorian era elaborate practice assaults against full-scale fortifications at Chatham were a popular public spectacle. A feature of many First World War training areas, and places where troops were accommodated, are practice trench systems. Some were relatively modest, while others, such as those on Salisbury Plain, Wiltshire, were as accurate representations of the Flanders battlefield as could be achieved. Mechanised warfare operated over much larger areas of land, and thus at sites like Elveden, Suffolk and Bovington, Dorset huge ranges were established for tank testing and training. Over 40 examples of practice trench systems are known, but many more await rediscovery (Fig 2.1). All provide physical evidence that care was taken to acquaint troops with trench routines and even rehearse operations.

At the outbreak of war in 1914 Britain had a relatively small regular army of just under a quarter of a million men; and in contrast to the large continental conscript armies, it was a volunteer army. The British army's main role was the defence of the Empire and large numbers were therefore stationed abroad. Late 19th-century military reforms led to the establishment of regimental base

depots in many county towns and volunteer forces formed strong local ties. While more specialised units, such as the Royal Engineers and Royal Artillery, had centralised depots, both at Woolwich, there were also volunteer engineer and artillery units based locally. The existing 123 or so barracks and depots were quickly overwhelmed by the influx of tens of thousands of volunteers. Initially, many were accommodated under canvas, but soon hutted camps sprang up composed of standard hut designs (Fig 2.2). Some were attached to existing

Figure 2.1 The remains of First World War trenches at Barry Buddon Training Centre, near Carnoustie, Tayside. The camp remains in use today (© Crown copyright: RCAHMS)

Figure 2.2 Summerdown Convalescent Camp, Eastbourne (Courtesy of Wayne Cocroft)

depots, while elsewhere, for example at Cannock Chase, Staffordshire, vast new camps the size of small towns appeared. Increasingly large number of prisoners of war also required housing; by 1918 about 164,000 were held in the UK. As with soldiers, at first ad hoc tented camps were established, which were later replaced with huts. Accommodation was also provided in converted premises as diverse as workhouses and unfinished textile mills.

Despite the British aversion to compulsory military service, the volunteer movement was strong and to accommodate their needs it has been estimated that there were over 2400 drill halls across the UK. Each local volunteer association was responsible for the provision of its own facilities. Some of the larger city and urban examples are very ornate and reflect the wealth and local pride of the units, while some grand rural halls were the gift of local magnates. In poorer areas the halls could be much more functional and basic; many also fulfilled the role of social clubs for their members. While few, if any, new drill halls were built during the First World War, many had close association with the units that mustered and were deployed both at home and overseas.

2.2 Drill halls

In 1908, the 'Haldane reforms' (named after Viscount Haldane, Secretary for War 1905–12), saw the merger of the various volunteer units – infantry, cavalry, artillery and engineers – to form the Territorial Force. The Territorial Force comprised some 268,000 men by July 1914 and this increased following the outbreak of war. By December 1915, when recruitment ceased, it numbered over 720,000 men.

However, concerns about the effectiveness of the Territorial Force at the outbreak of war led to the creation of a third element of the army – Kitchener's 'New Army'. These Territorial and New Army units were later affiliated with their local Regular Army unit, taking a higher battalion number. Thus the regular battalions might be 1st and 2nd, the Territorials 3rd and 4th and so on, with the New Army battalions taking the next number but with the addition of the title 'Service' (eg 6th (Service) Battalion).

This vast new force needed accommodation and local barracks and depots were unable to take the strain. The majority of the volunteer units were to be found in towns and cities where existing public buildings generally lacked spare capacity. Accordingly, 'drill halls' emerged as dedicated facilities for the Volunteer Forces and were once a common sight in almost every town and city in the country – a survey carried out by Mike Osborne in 2006 revealed 1863 documented examples in England alone. A similar survey in Scotland in 2013 identified no fewer than 340 drill halls, 288 of which were active in 1914.

Most volunteers were working-class labourers, both industrial and agricultural, and the units were, in the early days, private organisations with no access to central funds. Although many of the first volunteer groups adapted existing buildings such as village halls, where possible, a purpose-built drill

Figure 2.3 Golspie Volunteer Drill Hall. Built in 1892, in 1914 the hall became the Battalion HQ and base for A Company of the 5th Seaforth Highlanders (© RCAHMS)

Figure 2.4 Queen's Own Cameron Highlanders Barracks, Inverness (© RCAHMS)

hall was considered the most desirable option (Fig 2.3). However, as volunteers were responsible for paying for their own accommodation, the construction of purpose-built facilities was initially limited to those units best placed to raise the required funds.

During the First World War drill halls were where the Territorials met to be kitted out and mobilised – some volunteers served in Britain but most relieved regular garrisons in overseas territories or were deployed on active duty on the Western Front and in the Middle East. Whilst the war effectively put a stop to most new construction, drill halls became increasingly important as recruiting offices, training facilities, hospitals and mustering points, with a number of old buildings requisitioned to meet demand. However, many existing drill halls would have seen changes during the war and these may be significant, not only architecturally but also for their commemorative associations.

In Ireland, as in Britain, Regimental Depots were set up in towns in the recruiting areas. In 1914 these included the Royal Irish Regiment in Clonmel and the Royal Inniskilling Fusiliers in Omagh, while Belfast was the base for Royal Irish Rifles and the North Irish Horse. In Scotland, the depot for the Queen's Own Cameron Highlanders was the large Cameron Barracks in Inverness (Fig 2.4).

Design

The stylistic development of drill halls up to the outbreak of the First World War is characterised in England by the Gothick Revival and medieval-inspired 'toy castle' designs of the late 19th century. Examples include Grove (1874) and Bury (1868), which is possibly the epitome of this style and certainly one of the largest examples (Fig 2.5). North of the border the Scottish Baronial style was frequently used – a variant on the theme – although Arts and Crafts inspiration is also found. The domestic Tudor Revival style became increasingly popular around the turn of the century and was often combined with elements of the earlier

Figure 2.5 Bury Drill Hall (Lancs), opened in 1868 (© Katie Carmichael)

Figure 2.6 Oakham Drill Hall (Rutland), built 1914 (© Katie Carmichael)

castellated Gothick style, for example at Manchester, 1868; Ashton-under-Lyne, 1887; Southampton, 1889; and Bournemouth, 1895, before giving way to the neo-Baroque designs of the Edwardian period (eg Bilston, c 1902; Lancaster, pre-1913).

Drill halls became increasingly uniform in size and provision of facilities following the creation of the Territorial Force, with the commencement of a programme of building in 1907 which continued until the outbreak of war in 1914. Buildings of this period typically have a simple two-storey office block in front of the hall, often in the modified 'Wrenaissance' style which came to dominate the design of drill halls built in the years immediately prior to the outbreak of

Figure 2.7 The open hall of the York Road drill hall in Great Yarmouth, built in 1867. Although the use of laminated curved timber braces with finials is unusual, the provision of a viewing gallery at the end of the hall and the ridge light providing natural light are common features (© Katie Carmichael)

war (eg Hampton, Melton Mowbray, Oakham (Fig 2.6) and Shepshed, all built in 1914). Of course, not all drill halls can be ascribed to a particular style and many were simple, undistinguished, utilitarian structures with little or no architectural embellishment. As in the 19th century, many smaller drill halls of the early 20th century continued to be very plain buildings, with just hints of general historicist styles, as illustrated by Wolverton, also built in 1914.

Other than the mere huts, no two drill halls are truly identical, although groups deisgned by the same hand may be found, as for example a small group around Edinburgh associated with a Cycling Battalion. They do, however, all share three essential elements. These were combined to form a characteristic layout whereby the offices, armoury and stores were accommodated in an administrative block fronting the street, with a large open hall at right-angles behind (often with an indoor target range to one side and viewing balconies at either end) (Fig 2.7). The third element, accommodation for the caretaker or drill instructor, could be included within the administrative block or placed separately to the rear of the hall, as desired, but there are countless variations upon the basic layout.

In addition to their official military function, drill halls also acted as focal points for events within the wider community – many boasted of their suitability to host concerts, dances and meals – and some of the larger city drill halls were essentially private clubs for the middle classes, designed with dedicated social rooms and facilities such as billiard rooms, bars and reading rooms (Fig 2.8). Furthermore, drill halls also served a function in times of emergency

Figure 2.8 London and the larger cities contained a number of well-appointed drill halls which offered substantial social spaces, such as the lavishly furnished drawing room of 56 Davies Street, the HQ for the Queen Victoria and St George's Rifles (Reproduced by permission of English Heritage)

and during the war increasingly acted as training facilities, recruitment centres and mustering points. The drill hall of the 7th Royal Scots in Edinburgh acted as a makeshift mortuary to house the bodies of the many soldiers of the battalion who died in the Quintinshill rail disaster (see p68).

Adaptation and heritage values

Drill halls will be of interest to people for a variety of different reasons. Whilst they are frequently of evidential or aesthetic value, drill halls are especially important for their historical and communal values too – illustrative, associative, commemorative and symbolic, and will often have very strong local social value. Many drill halls also contain physical reminders of past lives and events in the form of battle honours and war memorials.

Adaptations and extensions to drill halls largely reflected the shifting demands made on the military and the volunteer forces over time. Wartime advances in technology and warfare had a significant impact not only on the organisation of the forces but also upon the architecture of their bases, with an increased focus on improved mobility and efficiency. Yeomanry units were rapidly converted into artillery and reconnaissance units, while the vast numbers of riflemen were replaced by fewer, smaller, more highly skilled units with access to armoured cars and lorries which needed garages. In addition, the development of anti-aircraft batteries and searchlight units all demanded large spaces with large doors for ready access. Although new drill halls were clearly preferable to meet these changing demands, many existing buildings will have been rapidly altered during and in the immediate aftermath of the war. These will inevitably have left physical clues to the changing situation, whilst unaltered examples suiting earlier requirements are also of interest.

2.3 Camps: temporary army training and prisoner of war

The outbreak of war, and the enthusiasm with which the general public responded to the government's call-to-arms, placed a considerable strain on the structure of the armed forces. The new conditions occasioned by a major European war, and the need to train men with little or no experience even in the Reserves, demanded a response on a hitherto unseen scale. Attempts to provide at least basic training demanded both the inventive use of existing infrastructure and the provision of new training camps. The camps that were established can be divided into three basic forms: tented and temporary accommodation; those that were adapted or taken over by the military from a previous purpose; and those purpose built. Many, if not most, camps would have incorporated two or even all three of these forms.

Circular bell-tents, of the type typically used for temporary training camps from the late 19th century, were commonly deployed in the weeks after

Figure 2.9 Bell tents
at Kilworth Camp,
Co Cork (Reproduced
by permission of the
National Library of
Ireland)

recruitment began in August 1914 (Fig 2.9). Tents were erected, for example, close to Heaton Hall, Manchester, to accommodate the volunteers, before they moved into purpose-built huts near one of the park lodges as winter set in. Tented accommodation is obviously the most difficult to locate archaeologically, but photographs can help in identifying locations, as recruits were eager to have their pictures taken in front of their new homes with their new comrades. The ground may have been levelled to take the tents, and on steeply sloping ground small drains or narrow rills were cut to direct draining water away from the tents. At Bron Aber, Transfynydd, a series of 20 concrete tent bases survives, terraced into the slope (Fig 2.10).

Figure 2.10 Recently
identified concrete
bases for bell tents at
Bron Aber, Gwynedd
(© Jon Berry)

By the end of 1914 timber huts were being built to accommodate recruits either at existing barracks or at new sites acquired by the military. The Leeds Pals battalion, for example, was sent into the Yorkshire Dales to a training camp in Colsterdale where reservoirs were under construction to supply the city. The associated navvy camp at Breary Banks was handed over by Leeds Corporation to the military and augmented with tents whilst extra huts were built that would eventually extend the site to over double its original size.

The essential features of a battalion training camp were around 44 communal living huts each holding 22–26 men plus NCOs, officers' quarters and mess, sergeants' mess, latrines, bath house, ablution blocks, stores, dining room, cook house and wash-up, guard room and offices. A standard camp layout with the huts arranged around a central parade ground was provided in the *Field Service Pocket Book* and in *Military Engineering vol VII: Accommodation and Installations* (Fig 2.11), but as with the construction of the huts themselves, it is clear that the plan was also adapted to suit local conditions and topography.

The standard hut was 60ft (c 18m) x 16–20ft (4.8–6m), timber-framed and raised above ground level (Fig 2.12). However, concrete floor pads are often the most apparent archaeological features, along with doorsteps and stove bases. At Colsterdale, where the huts were constructed perpendicular to the natural contours, the southern ends of the huts are marked by a level concrete floor, whilst the northern ends are marked out by concrete mounds formed around a timber post or foundation picket (3" x 3" (c 75 x 75mm) and 3" x 4" (c 75 x 100mm) for a corner picket) which supported the hut above ground level. Huts for enlisted men had a single central stove, whilst those for officers may have had three or more, providing a means by which to differentiate huts in photographs or indeed archaeologically. The huts were clad with a variety of materials including corrugated iron, tarred felt or timber boards. They had six windows on each side, with a hopper opening at the top, and doors in the gable ends, usually reached by two or three simple wooden steps, but on severe gradients, as at Skipton, a railed set of stairs and landing were necessary. The largest structures on site were the canteen and cook house. Centrally placed

Figure 2.11 A standard camp plan, from *Military Engineering, Accommodation and Installations*, HMSO 1934 (Courtesy of Jonathan Finch)

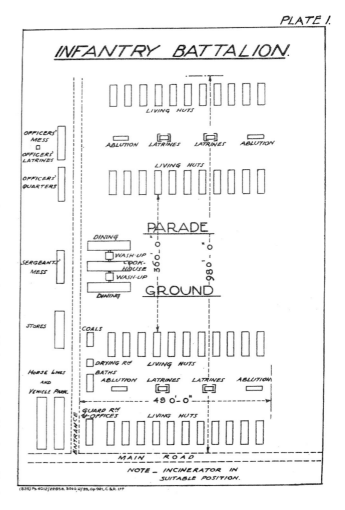

with louvred vents, several stove pipes, open lean-to and attached wash-up areas, the cook house was perhaps the most distinctive building and was near, if not attached to, the canteen or dining hall.

Brigade level camps, capable of taking thousands of men at a time, sprawled across the landscape. Brocton and Rugeley Camps were built on Lord Lichfield's estate at Cannock Chase and could accommodate up to 40,000 men, while Kinmel Park Camp at Bodelwyddan, Denbighshire was used to house the Canadian Expeditionary Forces. The densest concentration of training facilities was on Salisbury Plain which had been bought by the military for training purposes in the last years of the 1890s, and which swelled to accommodate the new army.

Infrastructure within the camps was essential and so water and sewerage systems, roads and electricity all had to be incorporated. Camps, including Ripon and Colsterdale, were often served by regular or narrow-gauge railways to facilitate moving building materials, supplies and men in and out of the camp. The scale of the larger camps also demanded more amenities including post offices, theatres, and hospitals. One of the key aspects of the camps is that the huts, structures and site sat within a wider landscape that was fully utilised for training and thus the surrounding area often contains related archaeological features. Two of the most identifiable are practice trench works and firing ranges.

A large number of British military camps in Ireland were established prior to the First World War as a direct result of the Boer War and the constant necessity of providing trained replacement troops to support the lengthy African campaign. Sites including Magilligan Musketry Camp, Ballykinler Rifle Range, and The Curragh and Kilworth Ranges were founded at the end of the 19th century on lands acquired by the War Department for this purpose. Due to the rapid development of Kitchener's New Army in 1914 an enormous expansion plan was drawn up for the British Army as a whole. This resulted in many of these previously established military centres in Ireland needing to be expanded to provide supplementary accommodation and training facilities for newly founded Irish Divisions. The expansions were augmented by the construction of various new training camps on land provided by the gentry on their country estates, at locations such as Clandeboye, Co Down; Randalstown, Co Antrim; and Lurgan in Co Armagh. In many cases these locations were already in use as drill grounds for the instruction of the newly formed ranks of Ulster Volunteers, founded in 1912 to oppose Home Rule in Ireland.

Prisoner of War camps

When the tide of war eventually began to turn in 1917 some training camps were transformed into camps to receive prisoners of war (PoWs), whilst civilian internment camps also began to receive PoWs. The rank and file were allotted, initially in small numbers and on a county basis in England, for agricultural, forestry and even land drainage work, whilst officers, in separate camps, engaged in sport and education without the obligation to work. The adjustments needed to the training camps were relatively slight – a double wire fence around the perimeter, with a patrol walk and double secure gates, carbide lights usually at the corners of the fence, and observation towers. Apart from additions to the perimeter of the camp there is usually little archaeological evidence of a change in function since the institutional needs of each were very similar. Cell blocks might be the only additional buildings needed. Although sports fields and more significantly vegetable and flower gardens were evident in the training camps, they became treasured assets within the PoW camps, as were the catering facilities such as the bakery, which could (under the limitations of rationing) produce the flavours and smells of home since they were run by prisoners. This occasionally

Figure 2.13 Stobs Camp, near Hawick, was first established in 1902. During the First World War it had both a training camp and a PoW camp, and it was further extended in the Second World War. The foundations of many of the buildings are still preserved (© RCAHMS)

had unexpected consequences: a guard at Stobs Camp noted 'We have five thousand German prisoners here and they have a better time of it than us. They bake all our bread, carving an Iron Cross on it. Some of the boys don't like it, but to my taste it seems all right.' The Imperial War Museum has republished a list of all places of internment issued by the Prisoner of War Information Bureau, but for many their exact sites still need to be located.

The huge military camp at Stobs in the Scottish Borders was used for training both before and during the First World War, but it also became the HQ of the PoW camp system in Scotland (Fig 2.13; see also Fig 1.6). A contract for 200 wooden huts was completed by the end of the winter of 1914–15 and as well as medical facilities the camp had a school, library and bakery. It also had a small cemetery for both military and civilian dead. It was reused and expanded for army training in the Second World War, finally housing the troops of the Polish Army prior to demobilisation in 1947–48. Although largely demolished, the building outlines are still clearly visible, and a number of the First World War buildings, including two of the PoW huts which can be identified on contemporary maps, survive.

There is evidence that in some cases PoWs were allocated to projects that could be deemed war work, such as the Germans sent to work at a large ironstone quarry on the island of Raasay, where they were accommodated in miners' cottages, or those at Beachley (Glos) who made the concrete blocks to construct workers' housing at National Shipyard No 1 in Chepstow. At Loch Doon, Ayrshire, over 1000 prisoners worked on the Loch Doon Aerial Gunnery School; this was clearly a military establishment and thus Britain was contravening the 1907 Hague Convention.

The end of camps

At the end of the war many of the new camps were decommissioned and the huts and structures were auctioned off to local farmers and villages, who were critically short of materials. The huts were reused as farm buildings, or even domestic structures, while frequently they found a new use as village halls, sometimes designated as 'Memorial Halls' to commemorate the community's sacrifice. Many village halls were renovated or replaced around the time of the millennium in 2000, resulting in the loss of several unrecognised survivals. One such hut-cum-village hall was recovered from Gayton to become the Cannock Chase Great War Camps Interpretation Centre in 2007 (see Fig 2.12), while at Cromarty, two huts removed from a nearby camp are now in use as holiday accommodation (Fig 2.15). An intact example has recently been identified at Craignethan Castle in Lanarkshire, where it is in use as a stonemason's hut, and a further example is the Hundleton Parish Reading Room in Pembrokeshire.

Identifying former camps is most readily done through searching local newspapers and archives, as their location was public knowledge. Events at camps, such as visits from local dignitaries, were regularly reported, as was the arrival or departure of men. The aristocracy was still relied upon to provide support in times of national emergency and so estate land (usually at a distance from the

Felday Prisoner of War camp

The investigation of the Felday Prisoner of War camp within the Iron Age hillfort of Holmbury St Mary, Dorking, Surrey by members of the Surrey Archaeological Society provides an excellent example of a small site-based research project combining field investigations and archival research. In 1917, the Royal Defence Corps established a camp, initially for 147 prisoners but rising to 208 in the following year. The prisoners were housed in standard 18m x 4.75m huts, each accommodating up to 30 men. They were employed by the local War Agricultural Committee felling timber. To assist in moving timber they laid patent Decauville narrow-gauge railway tracks with attached pressed steel sleepers. The investigation of the camp used standard archaeological methods of survey and specific targets were identified for excavation including a generator house, the floor slab of an unknown building and traces of temporary structures (Fig 2.14). In other areas dumps of calcium carbonate were discovered, a waste product from burning acetylene lamps. As is typical of many prisoner of war camps there are few documentary records, but fortunately recollections about the camp and a sketch by one of the village's older residents survived from the 1980s and a handful of photographs was also found. Another informative source was the Swiss Federal Archives and notes from attachés who had visited the camp on behalf of the Red Cross. A report of 21 May 1918 is typical:

Prisoners There are at present 208 German prisoners of war at this camp. Vizefeldwebel Karl Meerbote, (153. Inf. Reg.) is camp leader.

Description of camp The eight huts serving as dormitories are clean and well-

Figure 2.14 Members of the Surrey Archaeological Society surveying at Felday Prisoner of War camp within the Iron Age hillfort of Holmbury St Mary, Dorking (© Judith English & Jenny Newell)

kept and the dining room, which is now completed, offers ample accommodation.

Medical information A special hospital hut, with an RAMC orderly in attendance, is now in use. Dr Corby visits the camp twice weekly and when required. Serious cases of illness would be sent to Belmont War Hospital. The general health of the prisoners is good and they looked well and fit.

Work The work performed and wages received are the same as specified in the previous report (a penny a day).

Requests. Although the prisoners' quarters are good, and, on the whole, adequate, no bathing accommodation has as yet been provided – a serious inconvenience now that the hot weather has set in.

main house) was sometimes used, and records may be picked up in family and estate archives. However, as with Leeds, Sheffield and Manchester, civic pride was also an important driver and corporations preferred to use land they owned. Regimental histories and museums provide an excellent way to identify where training was undertaken and military publications, such as the *Field Service Pocket Book* or the multi-volume *General Specifications for Buildings and Works* can provide essential information about the organisation of sites and the standard structures to be found. Standing examples of camp structures are rare.

The process of demolition and removal is apparent archaeologically, with the foundation posts often sawn off just above ground level. Wooden posts and sills sometimes survive in damp conditions, but the most obvious remains are usually the concrete structural elements. These can include platforms for floors, bases for stoves, thresholds or doorsteps and the more substantial ablution and latrine blocks, and the bases of coal yards. Good examples of all these features may be found on Cannock Chase.

Figure 2.15 Two former army huts now converted to holiday cottages at Cromarty, near Invergordon (© Allan Kilpatrick)

Internment camps

In addition to prisoners of war, male civilians of military age of the enemy nations were interned. They were held across the country in special camps and also in segregated sections of prisoner of war camps. Two large camps were established on the Isle of Man, at Douglas and Knockaloe, near Peel; the latter held 25,000. At Ware, Hertfordshire, the existing German Farm Colony was used as a place of internment, as was Alexandra Palace. Extraordinarily, the National Sailors' and Firemens' Union ran a camp until October 1915 at Pattishall, Northamptonshire, for its German members serving on British merchant vessels.

After the end of the war Ballykinler British Army Training Camp became an official internment camp for Irish Republican Army (IRA) prisoners during the War of Irish Independence 1919–22. The camp had, however, already been used for political prisoners detained after the 1916 Easter Rising and for their involvement in the support given to the Irish nationalists by the German government. In 1916, and again in 1919, the camp was considered as a suitable location for the imprisonment of political prisoners, possessing numerous Armstrong huts fit and ready for habitation. These were later supplemented with some from The Curragh in County Kildare when Ballykinler took in detainees from other locations such as Kilworth, including IRA Volunteers and political activists. At the end of the Easter Rising in 1916, some 1800 Irish Republican prisoners were moved to Frongoch in North Wales where a former whisky distillery, originally occupied by German PoWs, was utilised as an internment camp.

2.4 Practice trenches and training remains

Military training has left physical remains of its fieldworks for centuries: Roman practice camps may be visited on the North Yorkshire Moors, in Dumfries and Galloway, and at Llandrindod Common and Gelli Gaer in Wales, while a unique set of earthworks in the Home Counties Training Area (Berkshire) date from 1792. More recent conflicts have seen the re-creation on British military training grounds of German anti-invasion defences from the Second World War, central European villages of Cold War vintage, and Iraqi and Afghan suburbs, all reflecting the conflicts of the 20th and early 21st century. The same is true of the Great War.

It is not true that the British military were unprepared for trench warfare, as examination of both the manuals available in 1914 and the equipment issued to soldiers shows. Trench warfare, with its use of blockhouses and machine-guns, had been a significant element in the siege of Port Arthur during the Russo-Japanese War, while bitter experience in the Boer War had taught the British the value not only of trenches, but also of their careful positioning and of an angled trace to reduce casualties from enfilading fire [incoming fire from an angle]. The 1908 War Office *Field Fortification Manual* presents examples of fieldworks that could be used to control ground and provide fixed positions for small arms fire. The value of entrenchment was further underlined by the inclusion of the pick-mattock [entrenching tool] as an element within the 1908 pattern webbing that was issued to all infantrymen. While the pick-mattock was not intended to create more than scrapes for immediate cover, the experience of 1914 showed how such temporary works could be extended and connected to create trench lines.

The training of both the Kitchener volunteers from 1914 onwards and the subsequent conscripts included significant elements designed to educate recruits in the construction, maintenance and use of trenches. In addition, the construction of field fortifications served not only to teach essential skills, but also improved body strength and fitness, developed team working, and created inter-personal bonds essential to effective soldiering: it has been noted that in the heat of battle a soldier fights not for flag, king, country or ideals, but for his mates. Nevertheless, the Great War was about more than infantry in trenches; it was a war characterised also by the use of artillery and by technological innovations, including tanks, machine-guns and chemical weapons, which have each left their distinctive marks on the landscape. Similarly, on Salisbury Plain and at Lulworth and Barry Buddon, the craters left by subterranean explosions provide graphic evidence of training for mine warfare.

Practice trenches

Practice trenches have been identified close to several army training camps and barracks. Examples of this direct physical relationship include Cannock Chase, Staffordshire, where extensive remains may be identified close to the site of Brocton and Penkridge Camps, at Seaford Camp in East Sussex, at Bodelwyddan, near Kinmel Park, and near the depot of the Royal Scots in the Pentland Hills, south of Edinburgh. In some cases trenches can be linked with particular units: examples at Blandford Camp, Dorset, were dug by men of the Royal Naval Division, while men of the 3rd Australian Division were responsible for some trenches on Salisbury Plain. However, in most cases the numerous detachments passing through the camps make individual unit connections uncommon, although particular regimental depots do have associated trenches, such as Lichfield. Nevertheless, research to identify the focus of a particular camp may indicate the uses to which trenches were put. At Otterburn, Northumberland, a trench system appears to have been built specifically as an artillery target, while trenches at Winterbourne Gunner, Wiltshire, including an unusual circular trench, were constructed specifically for training in the handling, release and testing of chemical weapons.

The ideal form of trenches may be seen in both plan and section in the various iterations of military manuals produced during and after the conflict. Typical features include lines of fire trenches, characterised by their regular, angled Greek Key trace, creating firebays (Fig 2.16). These trench lines, usually three

Figure 2.16 The recently identified network of First World War training trenches at Browndown, Hants, outlined on an RAF aerial photograph from 1951 (© English Heritage: RAF Photography)

deep, will often be connected to each other and to the rear area by more sinuous communication trenches. Both sorts of trench may also employ the upcast earth to create a parapet, thrown up in front of the trenches, and a parados, a bank on the reverse face. These served to increase the depth of the trench, giving more head cover, while the parados also afforded protection against shells bursting above and behind trenches. Although principally surviving as shallow earthworks, networks of trenches may be discernible in plan and on aerial photographs, where the different elements may be visible. The trenches may also exhibit different structural elements. For example, a fire trench should include a fire step on the forward face, which enabled the garrison to 'stand to' and see and fire over the parapet. Other fieldworks, in addition to the basic trenches, might include saps extending into no-man's-land from the front-line trenches, or bombing (grenade-throwing) and weapons pits excavated to the side of communication trenches. Saps could be used to listen for enemy activity, as sentry posts or for weapons, while pits between front, support and reserve trenches might serve a variety of uses, including for the positioning of trench mortars, similar to the examples shown in the 1916 film *The Battle of the Somme* or those excavated recently in Thiepval Wood. They may also have been used to provide positions for Lewis guns and bombers (troops specially trained with grenades) for close defence of trench systems in the event of enemy penetration. Positions for Vickers medium machine-guns may also be identified where training with this weapon was undertaken. Such positions could also house latrines! The standard trench plan, although set out in the various manuals, would be adapted to the local circumstances, including soil type and ground water – it was common in Flanders for trenches in low-lying areas to be built up (breastworks), rather than dug into wet ground and, where this was done, borrow (quarry) pits may be identified in front of trenches. Breastworks might also have been employed where the underlying geology made excavation difficult, such as on Penally's granite cliffs, or on the denser chalks of Salisbury Plain. It is also sometimes possible to identify whether the officers conducting training were taking account of the terrain: training trenches in Pullingshill Woods, close to Marlow, occupy the plateau above the valley and dominate it, as does a set above Oldacre Valley on Cannock Chase. Where the trenches are considered to be deliberately positioned within the landscape, study of both terrain and historic maps showing ground cover during the war may indicate whether 'enemy' trenches are likely to be present, or whether an impact area may be identified from grenade fragments or spent bullets. Specific grenade training trenches commonly resembled a capital E, with bays separated by earth bunds to shield men in the adjacent bay in case of accident, such as the well-preserved example at Rhicullen, near Invergordon.

When originally constructed, trenches would be revetted with a range of materials. These could include timber planking, wattle hurdles, sand bags, or expanded metal (XPM) or corrugated iron sheet, held in place with angle irons. A recent earthwork survey of trenches beside Dreghorn Barracks, Edinburgh, has revealed *in situ* corrugated iron sheets. In addition, other construction features may survive, including metal cables used for revetting, wooden trench boards (duckboards) or elements of 'A' frames, used to brace trench edges and support trench boards in wetter areas. Corrugated iron revetments will be readily apparent on geophysical survey, while preserved timber and the imprints of woven fabric from jute sand bags can be encountered during excavation.

On the battlefield itself, trench systems were permanently occupied and men often lived and worked underground, in dugouts and tunnelled shelters, although individual battalions would only spend a few days at the front at any one time, moving back to 'reserve' or 'support' positions, or to billets a mile or two away. The underground features are now difficult to discern at ground level, but one has recently been identified at Bodelwyddan practice trenches. Entrances may survive as slumped elements of trench lines and demolished or failed roofs will create hollows in the ground surface. Near Bulford, one dug out appears to have been created in a Bronze Age barrow [burial mound].

Trenches may have been dug singly to satisfy a single training objective, in more complex systems or, in the most developed cases, to replicate battlefields, complete with enemy positions and shell holes, as well as the Allied lines. The best-preserved, accessible British example is at Bodelwyddan Castle, in North Wales, while a similar, German example has been identified at Bovekerke, West Flanders. One such complex battlefield terrain was recreated at Bovington, Dorset, for tank training. This is the only currently identified re-creation of German defence in depth, which reached its epitome in the Hindenburg Line and is the subject of a detailed trench map; such battlefield sites also frequently included barbed-wire entanglements where the iron screw pickets may still survive, as they do near Shipton Bellinger, on Salisbury Plain.

Three divisions departed from Ireland to serve in the trenches during the course of the First World War, the 10th (Irish), 16th (Irish) and 36th (Ulster) Divisions. They were armed and trained in Ireland at a number of locations, with part of their training comprising instruction in methods of trench construction. The best examples of these practice/training trenches in Ireland can be seen at Ballykinler and Magilligan training camps in the north of the island and at The Curragh and Kilworth training estates in the south (Fig 2.17). Coincidently these landscapes are still managed by either the Ministry of Defence or the Irish Defence Forces. Other, less well-preserved examples exist at locations such as Phoenix Park in Dublin, and the Clandeboye estate in Co Down, associated in 1913 with the training of the Ulster Volunteer Army but which became a British Army camp in 1914.

Figure 2.17 First World War training trenches at Ballykinler, Co Down (© Heather Montgomery)

Particular use

The particular uses to which trenches were put may be identified from excavated evidence. At Otterburn, fuze caps dated to the First World War and associated shrapnel balls and splinters, all from shells, indicate use as a target, while grenade fragments at Colchester and Bodelwyddan demonstrate training in trench fighting. The presence of food tins and sauce bottles can be taken as an indication of use for training in trench routine over a period of days, but it should be remembered that trenches close to camps could also form ad hoc tips during decommissioning at the end of the war. In some cases, the origin and purpose of the trenches is known, including those at Bovington, while the Bustard trenches occupied by 3rd Australian Division were associated with a mine crater; both formed part of training specific to the imminent Battle of Messines. Two examples in central London also have identified origins: trenches on Clapham Common, visible on aerial photographs, are known to have been used for the proofing of trench mortars, which must have startled the man on the proverbial omnibus! Meanwhile, trenches in Kensington Gardens were used as part of the development of camouflage. Perhaps most unusually, the Loos Trenches at Poulton-le-Fylde, near Blackpool, were created by wounded servicemen and were open to visitors as a fund-raising mechanism for convalescent soldiers.

Miniature trenches

Not all identified practice trenches are at full scale. Examples on Cannock Chase include schematic three-line systems (Fig 2.18). One of these is associated with a large, levelled area considered likely to have been a hut base, suggesting an element of outdoor classroom/visual aid from the days before slides or computer imagery. However, the most remarkable example of miniature trenches is the Messines tactical model, also at Brocton Camp, where a 1:50 replica of the Belgian town of Messines and its German defences was created to train New Zealand troops in

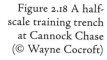

Figure 2.18 A half-scale training trench at Cannock Chase (© Wayne Cocroft)

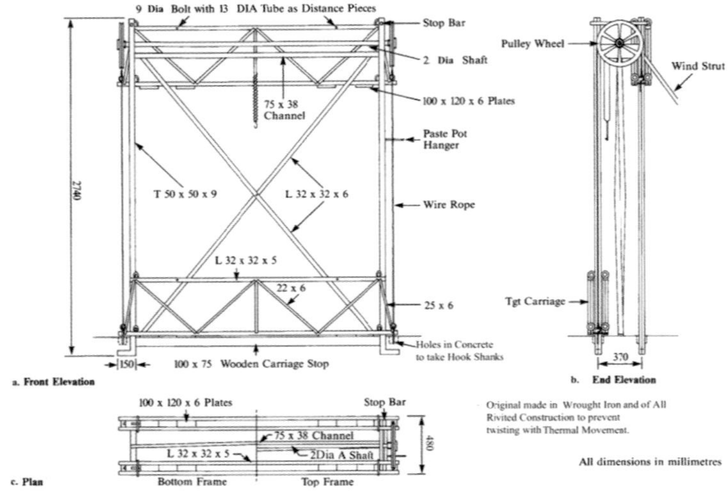

Figure 2.19a Hythe
Pattern Target
Frame: Plan

Figure 2.19b
Hythe Pattern
Target Frame:
view (© Heather
Montgomery)

1918. In each case, these miniatures afforded trainees the opportunity to achieve a
bird's-eye view of the trenches in order to improve understanding of a world that
would, at 1:1, be limited to views of trench walls, duckboards and the sky above!

In some cases the remains of firing ranges may be encountered. Plans or
descriptions of the types present at a site, such as the standard 100 yds rifle
range or Hythe Pattern Target Frames, may aid in the identification of remains
on the ground (Fig 2.19 a & b). At Penmaenucha, near Dolgellau, a fine group of
six Hythe Pattern Target Frames and marker's gallery survive *in situ*. Volunteer,
Territorial and Regular Army firing ranges can frequently be identified on
Ordnance Survey maps of the 19th and early 20th centuries.

2.5 Anti-invasion defence works

While a full-scale German invasion was not regarded as a threat in the way it was perceived to be in 1940, there were preparations to resist and repulse German landing parties. These included fieldworks planned around the port of Newhaven in East Sussex, surrounding Scraesdon Fort, Plymouth, and at the Royal Dockyard, Pembroke Dock. In addition, some parts of the late Victorian London Defence Positions Scheme were resurrected, with trenches connecting the Mobilisation Centres. It is their location that makes these fortifications more easily identifiable as defence works, rather than training aids. For example, the Seaford trenches are in dead ground behind Seaford Head with no obvious field of fire. Recent research has revealed that the eastern approaches to Edinburgh were defended by a continuous barbed-wire obstacle covered by strong points and firing trenches (Fig 2.20). The main coast defence batteries on the Forth estuary were also heavily defended with structures such as blockhouses and pillboxes; these features are clearly recorded on Royal Engineer maps at The National Archives, Kew.

Figure 2.20 Map showing the distribution of First World War trench systems on the Forth and Tay estuaries (© RCAHMS)

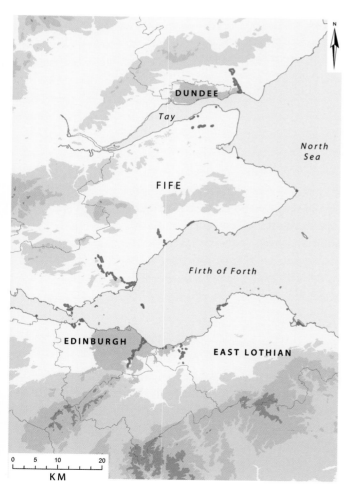

The majority of the anti-invasion defences were non-continuous, mutually supporting short lengths of fire trenches associated with barbed-wire entanglements, built as defended localities for a Section or up to a full Company strength, over-looking possible landing beaches (eg Felixstowe Beach), or up to Battalion and Brigade strength circling coastal towns and cities (Newcastle upon Tyne, Weymouth, Lowestoft, Dover etc). In some areas such as the Isles of Sheppey and Grain, the coast was very thickly prepared with a mixture of trenches, breastworks, redoubts, and blockhouses. Advanced linear defence lines (eg Swale to Detling), consisting chiefly of non-continuous trenches, blockhouses and pillboxes, supported by field and medium artillery batteries, were dug to obstruct the major routes to London, while the capital itself was protected by rings of defences that were based on the London Mobilisation Centres, built at the turn of the 20th century from Guildford, Surrey, to North Weald, Essex.

Some of these trench lines were quite

extensive but they were rarely as fully developed as those on the Continent; a number featured a fire trench and a reserve trench, but few formed a fully developed 'defence in depth', with three parallel successive lines of front-line, support, and reserve trenches linked by communication trenches. In addition to the coastal anti-invasion trenches and the in-land defence lines, strategic locations such as wireless stations, telephone exchanges, Trans-Atlantic and Empire telephone cable terminals, factories, waterworks, gasworks, power stations, railway tunnel portals and bridges were given their own defences to provide protection against saboteurs or attack, often with a blockhouse, guard hut, and wire entanglements.

In many cases these defences were modified or reused as part of the anti-invasion defences during the Second World War. Consideration of aerial photographs and maps may provide evidence of their existence prior to 1940, as has been the case at Seaford Head. The dating of anti-invasion defence works to a particular period of the First World War can be fraught with difficulty without documentary evidence, as the potential threat of invasion or raiding remained throughout the war and the various defences were subject to maintenance, re-construction, improvements, and strengthening. Great care needs to be taken when assessing the date of any earthworks or concrete structures, as First World War features can often be overlain by those dating from the Second World War (eg trenches at Shorncliffe, Kent, pillboxes at Auburn Farm and machine-gun posts at Spurn Point, both East Riding of Yorkshire). It is not an easy task and some sites can only be resolved by careful fieldwork and the use of documentary evidence or aerial photographs.

Trenches

A wide range of earthworks were excavated including fire and communication trenches, defence posts, redoubts, shelters, observation posts, machine-gun posts, and field-gun emplacements; all of these should be considered as the principal elements of the defences. Generally speaking, concrete structures should be viewed as an adjunct to the fieldworks, and hence any site with concrete structures should be examined for infilled or partially infilled earthworks and trenches existing nearby. A trench was always dug in stages and to a range of depths and profiles according to local needs, conditions and geology. Anti-invasion trenches were rarely as deep as those on the Continent, where the ideal depth was 8ft (2.4m). The form of these trenches mirrors that seen in the practice trenches.

Most anti-invasion trenches can be considered as little more than slit trenches, often no deeper than 3ft 9 in (1.1m) and 2ft (0.6m) wide, with the spoil from the trench either being thrown up to form a parapet in front of the trench, or used in sandbags. Where the ground was wet the trench was usually between 1ft (0.3m) and 1ft 6in (0.45m) deep and 3ft 6in (1.1m) wide; the parapet was between 2ft (0.6m) and 2ft 6in (0.75m) high. The volume of material necessary to build the parapet was often greater than could be obtained from the trench, so a borrow pit or trench might be dug to the front of the parapet to provide the extra volume of earth.

More fully developed trenches in dry ground were usually dug to a greater depth and width, providing more material for the parapet and parados. If the trench was deep or was intended to be occupied for any length of time the front and rear slopes would need to be revetted using a variety of materials – timber hurdles, planks, expanded metal sheets, corrugated iron sheets, wire hurdles, sods or sandbags. If the trench was longer than 18ft (5.5m), it would be traversed, ie dug to a plan (trace) similar in form to a crenellated castle wall, with 9ft (2.7m) wide traverses and up to 18ft-wide fire bays. The traverses projected back across the line of the trench to prevent shell splinters and bullets travelling along its length. In addition to the crenellated plan, trenches could have a sinuous curved trace without traverses, dog-legs, tenallie (zig-zag) or bastioned traces.

Strong points or redoubts would be dug where the ground gave good command over surrounding territory. A strong point consisted of a discrete complex of mutually supporting trenches, machine-gun posts and shelters, within a barbed-wire perimeter, usually with a 360° field of fire and the ability to provide flanking fire to the approaches of the adjacent front-line fire trenches. The machine-gun posts could vary in appearance and construction, some being little more than a 1ft 6in (0.45m) deep, 3ft (0.9m) by 4ft (1.2m) wide platform cut into the parapet of a trench with a narrow 3ft-long (0.9m) trench on its right-hand side. They could be given overhead protection by layering earth onto a timber or corrugated steel ceiling, and as time went on, many such posts were replace by concrete pillboxes. Field gun emplacements for 12-pounder and 15-pounder guns were sometimes dug to the rear of the trenches, often in woodland. These took the form of shallow trapezoidal or rectangular plan pits with sloping floors, some with a curved recess to accept the rear spade on the trail of the gun carriage. The spoil from digging the pit was used to form a parapet on three sides but the rear was left clear to allow the gun to be withdrawn if necessary.

Today many trenches survive as infilled features in the modern landscape and can only be recognised as slight hollows in the ground or as areas of differential plant growth, where plants can grow more vigorously. In other places levelled trenches present a distinct pattern on air photographs. Nevertheless, some trenches dating to the First World War can still be found surviving in areas where the land has not been cultivated, on moorlands or in woodlands. At Hedderwick Links, part of the anti-invasion defences of the Forth estuary, some 750m of trenches survive up to 1m deep in places, along with the site of a redoubt, machine-gun posts and a communication trench. The emplacing of field guns in woodlands means that the emplacements may also survive where the woodland hasn't been felled or replanted since the First World War (eg Waverley Forest, Norfolk). The recent identification in Fife of ringworks, previously classified as prehistoric, as being banks of soil around First World War blockhouses demonstrates the importance of using a variety of sources, such as historic maps and aerial photographs, both old and new.

Breastworks

Where the ground was unsuitable or where there was a high water-table, the defences had to be built up as sandbagged breastworks. At many locations sandbag structures such as barricades, machine-gun posts, and blockhouses were often the only structures built; such ephemeral sandbag features will now be long gone but sometimes, if the ground hasn't been disturbed, sufficient sand was deposited out of the sandbags that the shape of the structure or breastwork can still survive today as a low grassy feature (eg the defence post, Slade Cross, Cosheston, Pembrokeshire).

Concrete fortifications

Both reinforced and mass concrete was used to build observation posts, defence posts, gun emplacements and pillboxes; these structures were, therefore, more durable from the outset and many were re-occupied during the Second World War, as for example those surviving at Auburn Sands, Bridlington. The most common type of First World War anti-invasion structure to survive is the pillbox, so called due to their similarity in appearance to the little white cardboard boxes used by pharmacists to dispense pills, although it is clear some which were designed to defend coastal batteries, eg Aberdeen, were built before 1914. Unfortunately, the true identity and historic value of these structures is often not appreciated and they are frequently misidentified as belonging to the Second World War, being 'two a penny', and are lost through ignorance and a lack of care (Fig 2.21). An example at RAF Sealand is now thought to be of First World War date, rather than Second, on the basis of aerial photographic evidence.

There is no ready way to determine First World War pillboxes from those produced during the Second World War, unless documentary evidence is used to try and establish a particular design or nuance to the period, or there is physical evidence such as one at North Berwick which has '1919' inscribed in the concrete. There were round, square, rectangular, ovoid, regular hexagonal and lozenge plan pillboxes built in both world wars. Variations in regional distribution of types does however occur and can be an aid to identification – circular-plan

Figure 2.21 The First World War pillbox at St Olave's Bridge, Norfolk, with a later structure added on top (© R J C Thomas)

pillboxes are more commonly found in Norfolk and Suffolk, square-plan in the East Riding of Yorkshire, hexagonal and ovoid in Kent, and lozenge-plan with rounded corners defending coast artillery batteries. A wide variety of designs and plan-forms were produced: some were little more than thin-walled concrete linings, intended to support a sandbag covering, whereas others were designed from the outset to be shell or splinter-proof.

Obstacles

Virtually all anti-invasion defences were protected by barbed-wire entanglements. These entanglements could vary dramatically in scale and form, including single aprons, double aprons, trip fences, low wire, high wire, coils of wire, and all manner of combinations. The entanglements were held in place by timber posts, iron posts, angle-iron pickets and screw pickets. Unless buried, it is unlikely that any First World War entanglement survives today; however, picket posts do survive, but once again, identical ones were used during the Second World War and consequently it is difficult to date such features unless they are part of a known site.

One aspect often forgotten is the clearance of woodland and hedgerows to open up fields of fire for the defences; evidence for such clearances may still be found in the landscape where differential hedge growth can be observed. Lengths of cleared hedges situated adjacent to public roads or at road junctions were sometimes replaced during the 1920s by steel deer park fencing, rather than by replanting the hedge; such fencing can be indicative of clearances, but care must be taken not to jump to conclusions.

Camps

To begin with the soldiers manning the anti-invasion defences were generally accommodated in bell tents, but as the war dragged on, it became clear that it was unreasonable to house men at exposed coastal sites during the autumn and winter months under canvas. Isolated locations like the marine telephone cable terminal at Abermawr, Pembrokeshire, were provided with a single guard hut to give the soldiers protection from the elements, but the more substantial linear anti-invasion defences were provided with a number of hutted camps varying in size from company strength (227 officers and men) up to a full battalion (1007 officers and men).

2.6 Hospitals

Prior to the war, there were 7000 military hospital beds; by the end there were 364,133, including over 13,000 for officers. With very few purpose-built hospitals set up during the First World War (Fig 2.22), this huge increase was achieved in a number of ways, ranging from the use of existing hospital facilities to the establishment of hospitals in buildings such as stately homes, village halls and

Figure 2.22
Invergordon Naval
Hospital under
construction. Built
to serve the large
naval base, this is a
rare example of a new
hospital constructed
during the war
(© RCAHMS:
Invergordon Album)

large public buildings (Fig 2.23). Major civilian hospitals allocated beds for military casualties, caring for those who had received a 'blighty' wound. 'War Hospitals' were established in large public buildings, for example Scotland's No 1 Military Hospital in Aberdeen occupied four schools and a poorhouse. Purpose-built poorhouses and asylums were ideally suited and many did not return to their original function after the war (eg the Western General in Edinburgh).

A significant proportion of hospital and convalescent beds were provided by local voluntary effort, supported by the Red Cross. Over 1600 'auxiliary hospitals' were established in premises ranging from stately homes to village halls. The precise identity of many of these hospitals has not been established, although some bear plaques recording their use. Local newspapers frequently reported fund-raising events, and the decorations awarded to their medical and nursing staff are recorded in the pages of the *London Gazette*.

Figure 2.23 The
Aston Webb building
at the University
of Birmingham
which served as the
Southern General
hospital (© University
of Birmingham)

This use of established buildings means that there are very few ruins of hospitals from the First World War which people can explore. Yet there are a number of legacies from the war that can be seen in buildings around the country, including stately homes and some of the large hospitals.

Stately homes

Stately homes were very useful for housing large numbers of patients and required very little in the way of modification. The principal rooms were perfect for wards and the sizeable kitchens and laundries were accustomed to catering for the needs of large groups of people. As country estates were becoming more expensive to run, many owners of stately homes were quite willing to give up their houses, and it was also a way for them to support the war effort. Roehampton House, a stately home in south-west London which was opened in 1915 for the treatment of amputees and the provision of artificial limbs, is still standing, although the main building that housed the many patients has been converted into private luxury apartments (Fig 2.24). The lodge gates are also still standing. Another stately home, Erskine House, near Glasgow in Renfrewshire, became the Princess Louise Hospital for Limbless Sailors and Soldiers in 1916 and was the second

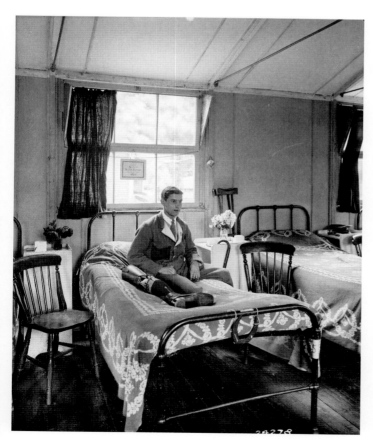

Figure 2.24 An amputee recovering at Roehampton Hospital (Reproduced by permission of English Heritage)

largest limb-fitting hospital in Britain after Roehampton. Erskine House is still standing and it is now the 5-star Mar Hall Hotel. Another stately home, Nocton Hall in Lincolnshire, was given to the United States Army in 1917, when the United States entered the war, and was used as a convalescent hospital for injured troops. The site is now derelict and therefore dangerous to enter, but the building, although fenced, can be clearly seen from the perimeter.

One of the most iconic buildings used for housing the war wounded was the Royal Pavilion in Brighton. Designed by John Nash for George IV, its magnificent interior is a reflection of his personality and Regency reign. From December 1914 to February 1916, the Royal Pavilion was used as a hospital for wounded troops from the Indian Corps. Its oriental exterior was thought to make the Indian soldiers recover more quickly as they were amongst familiar surroundings. The Pavilion is still very much a part of the architectural scene in Brighton, and is open to visitors.

Many stately homes have exhibitions that relate to the house and its role during the First World War, where visitors can see images and explore the site further. Examples include Blenheim Palace, Oxfordshire; Dunham Massey, Cheshire; and Wrest Park, Bedfordshire. Paintings, archive photographs, contemporary accounts and film footage are part of a permanent exhibition at the Brighton Pavilion.

Military hospitals

One of the most interesting sites for exploration is the Royal Victoria Hospital in Netley, Hampshire. Although construction began on the military hospital in 1856 at the suggestion of Queen Victoria, Netley Hospital had an important role in the First World War when many wounded men were housed there. The largest military hospital in Britain, it was a quarter of a mile (435m) long, had 138 wards and approximately 1000 beds. An asylum was built at the back of the hospital in 1870 and an extension erected in 1908 (Fig 2.25). This housed the notorious D Block, where many of the men suffering from the traumatic emotional effects of the First World War, often known as 'shell-shock', underwent treatment.

Figure 2.25 Aerial view of Netley Hospital, Hants taken in 1923. The remains of the additional hutted accommodation erected during the war can be seen on the right
(© English Heritage: Aerofilms Collection)

Figure 2.26 The UVF hospital wing at Queen's University Belfast, 1915 (Courtesy of the Somme Museum)

This building still stands and is now the Hampshire Constabulary Police Training Headquarters. While the main hospital building was severely damaged by fire in 1963 and demolished in 1966, some buildings do remain. The officers' mess, which was built separately, is now private apartments. Of the main hospital, the only building still standing is the chapel, which was preserved. Now located in the Royal Victoria Country Park, the chapel is open to visitors and has an exhibition telling the history of the hospital.

Craiglockhart in Edinburgh has become one of the best known military hospitals as a result of the pioneering work of Dr William Rivers in treating shell-shock victims; his patients included the war poets Siegfried Sassoon and Wilfrid Owen. Built originally as a hydropathic establishment in the 1880s, the run-down buildings were absorbed into the military medical system. The main building is today part of Edinburgh Napier University.

In 1914 the Ulster Volunteer Force (UVF) offered their entire medical facilities to the War Office. This was supplemented in 1915 when the UVF hospital was opened in Exhibition Hall, a building adjoining Queen's University which was donated by Belfast Corporation (Fig 2.26). Further UVF hospitals were established in Co Down at Dunbarton House, Gilford and Craigavon House.

Mount Stewart House, situated on the shore of Strangford Lough, was offered to the Admiralty for use as a Naval Hospital from 1915 to 1919 by Augusta, Lady Bute, wife of the 7th Marquess of Londonderry.

Commemoration in hospitals

One of the lasting legacies of war is the many sites of commemoration. Doctors, professional nurses, porters, and Voluntary Aid Detachments were all killed during the war, and memorials to the dead can often be found in the hospital chapel. Several of the large hospitals in London such as St Bartholomew's, St Thomas's, Guy's and King's have memorials or plaques that commemorate the war dead, ranging from small plaques to larger memorials such as the Elder Memorial Chapel at the Western Infirmary, Glasgow. At King's College Guy's Campus in London, a Portland stone memorial arch designed by William Walford, unveiled by the Duke of York in July 1921, sits in the Memorial Park. At St Bartholomew's, a plaque set in the east wing of the square highlights the hospital's role in the care of those in the British Expeditionary Force. Memorials can also be found in many regional hospitals where the war wounded were cared for, or where medical personnel are remembered for their work in the war.

CHAPTER 3

Life on the Home Front

3.1 Introduction

Throughout Queen Victoria's reign Britain's civilian population felt secure behind the wooden walls of the Royal Navy and strong coastal defences; war was a distant event played out on the fringes of Empire and reported in illustrated newspapers. The First World War shattered this wellbeing and brought conflict to Britain's shores; German warships, and even submarines, bombarded coastal towns, and airships and aircraft brought death and destruction from above (Fig 3.1). In coastal waters shipping and fishing vessels were threatened by mines and U-boats. These threats, patriotic fervour, and outrage at reports of German atrocities as they invaded Belgium and France encouraged men to enlist in vast numbers. As more and more men were drawn into the armed forces, especially after 1916, women filled the gaps in the workforces of the railways, urban transport, and industry, as well as on the land.

But it would be too simplistic to present a picture of a population totally behind the national war effort for its duration. There were those who opposed the war on moral grounds and refused to serve in the armed forces, many of whom were imprisoned, while others served bravely in ambulance units. Immigrant communities from the enemy powers, in particular Germans, Austrians and Turks, were subject to open hostility, and men of military age interned. In industry, new working methods and resentment against perceived war profiteering created industrial discontent leading to strikes: in the south Wales coalfield, some 200,000 miners went on strike in 1915. In Ireland demands for independence continued, culminating in 1916 in the outbreak of civil war and treasonable dealings by the Irish nationalists with the Germans; this led in the winter of 1917–18 to the replacement of all Irish Territorial troops in Ireland with Scottish Territorial troops due to concerns over their loyalty. After the war's end dissatisfaction with the pace of demobilisation spilled over into army mutinies. Only in very rare instances will physical traces of dissent be found, such as the graffiti left by conscientious objectors imprisoned in Richmond Castle.

As the armed forces grew in size they created a huge demand for war *matériel* of all types. They required mundane items, such as uniforms, boots, and pots and pans. This demand could be met largely by existing manufacturers halting production for the civilian market and working their factories more intensively. Some specialist items, for example shells, were made in existing engineering works. Over 6000 essential factories were classified as Controlled

Establishments, where working conditions were controlled and workers were required to apply for permission to leave. Just over 200 factories were directly managed by the government and were known as National Factories.

Virtually every building constructed before 1918 will have a story to tell about its occupants, perhaps of a soldier who left for war or a woman engaged in war work. Many of those who remained at home were keen to contribute to the war effort; women joined voluntary nursing organisations and often led charities dedicated to assisting refugees or providing comforts for troops and prisoners of war. There were few resources to construct new buildings, requiring organisations to set up their headquarters in existing buildings.

Britain's railways played a crucial role in transporting troops, moving munitions and goods to supply the Western Front, and sea mines to defend the North Sea shipping lanes. Partly assembled mines manufactured in the US were landed at Corpach and Kyle of Lochalsh on Scotland's west coast and

Figure 3.1 Damage caused to the barracks at Scarborough Castle during the bombardment of 16 December 1914 (Reproduced by permission of English Heritage)

transported to the US Naval mine bases at Inverness and Invergordon via the Caledonian Canal and by rail respectively. This huge effort on the railways was largely achieved through the more intensive use of the existing network. In some places temporary wooden extensions were made to existing platforms and short links added to make more efficient use of some junctions. At most new munitions factories and large army camps extensive sidings and internal lines were added, although few survived the end of the war. Similarly, the canal system was used where possible to move war *matériel*, but at that time the system was badly run-down and there was little new construction work.

As German U-boat attacks on merchant shipping increased, the import of war *matériel* and as importantly, food supplies, was directly threatened. To counter this, the countryside was mobilised for war: land was used more intensively and marginal areas were brought under the plough. The ability of farmers to increase production was curtailed by the loss of men to the armed forces, a factor partly offset by the formation of the Women's Land Army in 1917, mechanisation, and the employment of PoWs. In urban areas, army camps, and even within munitions factories, allotments supplemented food supplies. The war created huge demands for timber and in some areas specialist Canadian lumberjacks assisted in tree felling.

The Easter Rising 1916

The Easter Rising was a pivotal event in Ireland's recent history: an armed insurrection staged during Easter week 1916, by Irish Republicans with the dual aims of ending British Rule in Ireland and establishing an independent Irish Republic. The uprising took place at a time when the United Kingdom was fully absorbed by the war and the supply of arms to the IRA by the Germans was seen as a major threat by the British government. The events of the Rising have been extensively recorded and are now well represented in both literary and pictorial terms. These can be used to inform tours of some of the main locations involved in the events of Easter 1916. In addition to the General Post Office (Fig 3.2) these include the Four Courts, a strategic location during the Rising, controlling the main routes between the military barracks and the General Post Office. The Jacobs Biscuit Factory (now the repository of the Irish National Archives) operated as a stronghold, and Wellington Barracks (now occupied by Griffith College) was a British Army recruitment and training centre. Trenches were reportedly dug on St Stephen's Green in a bid to prevent any possible access by the British Army. The uprising ended at No 1 Moore Street with the surrender of the Council of the Irish Republican Army. A campaign is ongoing to protect the historic Moore Street area of Dublin from redevelopment in the hope of safeguarding the entire terrace and surrounding lanes at Moore Street as a National Monument. Many buildings were destroyed during the insurrection, while others have long since been demolished or remodelled. Some locations do survive at least in part and can provide a fascinating tangible and supplementary narrative as to how the Rebellion unfolded, telling the story of a very different Dublin 100 years ago.

Figure 3.2
The Dublin
GPO building
(© Wayne Cocroft)

3.2 Industry

At the outbreak of war, the country's armaments industry was organised to supply a relatively small peacetime army, one mainly concerned with policing the Empire. By autumn 1914 the war had stagnated into static trench lines stretching from the Belgian coast to Switzerland. In an attempt to break these lines it was argued that huge quantities of high-explosive shells were required. Initially, existing factories were expanded, including the Royal Gunpowder Factory at Waltham Abbey, as were private explosives works, such as those at Cliffe, Kent, and Nobel Explosives at Pembrey, the first purpose-built TNT factory which was established in 1914. Elsewhere, local engineering works joined together to form shell committees. Their premises varied from well-equipped railway and tramway workshops to a toy factory and a herring-curing works. By early 1915 it was evident that existing systems were inadequate to produce the huge quantities of war *matériel* required, the so-called 'shells scandal' of early 1915 highlighting the lack of capacity within the existing state factories and ad hoc local committees. Consequently, in June 1915 the Ministry of Munitions was established under Lloyd George, with the eventual creation of over 200 National Factories (Fig 3.3). The main government armaments factories were at the Royal Arsenal, Woolwich, the Royal Small Arms Factory, Enfield, and the Royal Gunpowder Factory, Waltham Abbey. A Royal Balloon Factory had been established at Farnborough in 1912, and in 1914 the Royal Naval Cordite Factory at Holton Heath, Dorset was approved. Prior to this, the sole substantive supplier of acetone, the solvent required for cordite,

Figure 3.3 Aerial view of the National Projectile Factory, Hackney (© English Heritage: Aerofilms Collection)

was the Wood Distillation Works at Coleford, Forest of Dean, established in 1913. However, the 'largest factory in the world' was to be established in 1915 on the Solway Firth: measuring eight miles by two miles, HM Factory, Gretna produced cordite for shells. It employed 19,000 people (around two-thirds of them women) and produced 800 tons of explosives a week. The site was decommissioned after the war, but at least eight of the wooden huts built to house the workers are known to survive. Meanwhile the vast Nobel explosives factory at Ardeer in Ayrshire was felt to be so vulnerable to attack from the sea, it had its own coast artillery battery and machine-gun-defended perimeter.

Many of the technologies that are associated with the war, including aircraft, airships, wireless communications, and submarines were all products of the preceding decades. All were given a boost by the war: in 1914 just 50 aeroplanes were produced per month; by 1918 this had risen to 2700 per month, built in factories as far north as Aberdeen where, in the absence of a suitable aerodrome, they were transported south by rail. The war also created the demand for new products, ranging from respirators or gas masks to portable telecommunications equipment and tanks. New products were often produced by existing manufacturers: airship components were made by shop fitters, waterproof garment makers, sculptors and agricultural instrument makers. Likewise, essentially wooden aircraft were produced in former furniture factories, although three purpose-built National Aircraft Factories were constructed, along with larger works for the leading aircraft manufacturers.

Construction materials

A wide range of materials was used to construct the new munitions works. Most factories followed contemporary building techniques and were brick-built with roofs supported by light steel trusses. The roof type most commonly associated with the war was the Belfast truss (Fig 3.4). This roof form used relatively short lengths of wood and could be assembled by semi-skilled workers. At Cliffe explosives works, Kent, the press houses, acetone recovery stoves, and cordite stores were built from reinforced concrete (Fig 3.5). These are a rare example and elsewhere concrete was used infrequently, although concrete blocks are encountered. For speed of construction various types of timber-framed buildings were utilised, clad in materials such as weatherboards, corrugated-iron, and asbestos cement sheets. Within works, names on bricks may indicate the source of building materials, as may other surviving marked building fittings and plant (Fig 3.6). The purpose-built factories were able to utilise the relatively new power source of electricity, both to power machinery and to provide artificial light. In common with many pre-war industrial concerns the new factories were often given architecturally distinguished administrative buildings; one of the most impressive is the three-storey neo-Georgian frontage to the National Machine-gun Factory at Burton-on-Trent (Fig 3.7).

Figure 3.4 Large coupled shed at RAF Leuchars with a
Belfast truss roof (© RCAHMS)

Figure 3.5 Cordite magazine built of reinforced concrete at the
Cliffe explosives works in Kent (© Wayne Cocroft)

Figure 3.6 Bricks with the manufacturer's name stamp
(© Wayne Cocroft)

Figure 3.7 The entrance to the former National Machine Gun Factory site
at Burton-on-Trent, now a B&Q store (© Wayne Cocroft)

Engineering works

Prior to the war the Royal Arsenal at Woolwich was the main state heavy armaments works and along with private producers, such as the Coventry Ordnance Works, their workshops shared many of the characteristics of their civilian counterparts, including administrative and drawing offices, forges, presses, and erecting shops with overhead cranes. The Admiralty had commissioned a vast torpedo factory to be built at Greenock in 1910, within the heavy gun defences of the Clyde. In Lincoln, William Tritton & Co Ltd, agricultural engineers, made a seamless move to tank manufacture. Steel shells of all sizes were forged in various foundries, including Blaenavon in south Wales; the initial steel forgings were then taken for machining on lathes to fine tolerances controlled by gauges. Railway workshops were ideal for this work and many undertook shell production (Fig 3.8). Elsewhere, purpose-built shell and projectile works were built.

Initially, existing works were extended, but new capacity was also needed. In the new purpose-built works, such as the Lancaster National Projectile Factory, modern principles of scientific management as espoused by Frederick W Taylor in America were applied. Large open workshops allowed production to be organised in logical flow-lines with enough flexibility to be reconfigured for new products. By a process known as 'dilution' complex tasks were broken down to be performed by unskilled or semi-skilled labour; and from about 1916 often by women.

The locations of most of the large munitions works are known. Less well known is the role of many smaller, local engineering works. These smaller works often made important contributions to the war effort, such as one in Banbury that devised an innovative machine for filling mustard gas shells. Accounts of this war work may be found in contemporary newspaper records or company histories, many of which had a local and restricted distribution.

Figure 3.8 Railway workshops were ideal for the manufacture of both guns and munitions. This image is of the North Eastern Railway Shell Shop at Darlington

Few munitions factories existed prior to the First World War in Ireland; however Kynoch in Arklow, Co Wicklow (est 1895) was already manufacturing cordite (Fig 3.9), and so expanded to meet the demands of war. By 1917 five National Factories had been established in Ireland, at Cork, Dublin (2), Galway and Waterford which were producing various essential munition components.

Chemical works

Figure 3.9 Cordite recovered during excavations at Thiepval Wood by the Somme Association (© Heather Montgomery)

Given the significance of the chemical industry, it has received comparatively little attention from industrial archaeologists. Obsolete chemical plant is usually quickly cleared, although front offices may survive. Where explosives works survive as earthworks and ruins, the foundations of their chemical sections may reveal some evidence of former processes. Broken earthenware may also be found offering further information on processes and suppliers. The past activities on these sites mean the ground should not be disturbed without a thorough risk assessment. While few traces of the First World War chemical industry now remain, most sites will be identifiable from maps of the 1920s and may be visible on the online *Aerofilms* collection.

By the beginning of the 20th century Britain had become dependent on German chemical imports, especially dyestuffs and specialised chemicals such as acetone and sulphuric acid. These chemicals were essential to the war effort and the dyestuffs technology based on coal tar derivatives was also vital for the production of toluene and phenol, the precursors of the high explosives TNT and Lyddite. Many of these works were associated with the textile industry in the north-west of England, and the chemical industries of the Thames estuary and central Scotland. Later in the war the skills of the organic chemists were applied to the production of poison gases.

Filling factories

The production of a typical single shell involved bringing together components from a number of factories including the steel shell, brass cartridge case, and brass fuze assemblies. In turn these needed filling with a variety of explosives, propellant charges, disruptive high explosives, and sensitive initiation compounds. A number of serious accidents occurred including one at Chilwell, Nottighamshire which killed 134 people (Fig 3.10). In the filling factories many

of the buildings were small, specialised and contaminated, and the majority were cleared at the end of the war. Survivals may still be found of the less-specialised buildings which could be converted to new uses. Elsewhere, traces of the National Filling Factories at Banbury (Northamptonshire), Barnbow (West Yorks) and Georgetown (Renfrewshire) survive as earthworks which are reminiscent of the remains of deserted medieval villages.

Figure 3.10 The wreckage of the National Shell Filling Factory at Chilwell, Nottinghamshire, after an explosion on 1 July 1918 which killed 134 people and injured 250 (Reproduced by permission of English Heritage)

Textiles and related industries

As a direct result of the war, Ireland saw a marked increase in demand for linen, mills such as Herdman's Linen Mill at Sion Mills, Co Tyrone being provided with a much-needed boost to their pre-war dwindling flax industry. Flax was needed to be spun into the crucial commodity of tough specialist linen for the manufacture of aircraft wings; elsewhere many other mills and shirt factories were hard-pressed furnishing the increasing demands of military contracts for items such as tents, bandages, and army bedding. The demand for blankets and uniforms was to reinvigorate the woollen industry in both Ireland and Wales. Other, smaller contracts were issued to factories such as the Enniscorthy Agricultural Co-operative for leather accessories.

Welfare

Some 6000 factories considered vital for the prosecution of the war effort were designated as Controlled Establishments. Within these establishments restrictions were placed on the movement of labour and industrial action, and wages were controlled. One of the positive effects of the war was the promotion of new welfare standards. Partly due to the remoteness of some factories, this included the provision of canteens. It was believed that social facilities would discourage excessive drinking in and around some munitions plants and at places like Enfield and Carlisle (near the huge explosives factory at Gretna) and around the Invergordon Naval Base pubs were brought under state control. In the new factories canteens were routinely incorporated into their design, along with facilities such as washing and changing areas. Other establishments were provided with more basic facilities, such as mess rooms and plumbed toilets. These buildings, which could be easily reused, often survive.

Housing

The creation of new munitions factories, often in remote locations, resulted in the displacement of tens of thousands of people all of whom needed housing. Across the country the Ministry of Munitions constructed around 10,000 permanent houses, along with many temporary cottages and hostels (Fig 3.11). At virtually

Figure 3.11 Between 1916 and 1918 John Laing and Sons was contracted to build houses, a post office, a hospital, an employment exchange, a bank, shops, a police station and the All Saints Episcopal Church as part of the Gretna Township which was created for the workers of the munitions factory, HM Factory, Gretna (© English Heritage: John Laing Collection)

750. 24. 2. 19. GRETNA. CINEMA & SHOPS.

Munitions workers' housing: Mancot

Mancot Royal, Flintshire, was built to house about 7000 key workers and their families for the Queensferry Explosives Factory on the south bank of the Dee Estuary. The majority of the workforce commuted by train, but chemists and the police needed to be housed on site. The site architect was Theodore Fyfe, formerly employed by Sir Arthur Evans at Knossos and later an academic at Cambridge, but here he was under the overall direction of Raymond Unwin, the Socialist architect and town planner. There are similarities in detail with other Ministry of Munitions sites such as Gretna, but also with subsequent local authority estates. About 180 houses were built in local light-red brick, roofed with Welsh slate, while hostels designed for post-war conversion to separate houses accommodated 84 single workers including the women police who were responsible for security and safety amongst the female workers. Houses included some larger ones, with distinctive gable-end chimneys, for supervisory grades, as well as semis and groups of three or four. Sash or casement windows were further status indicators, while triple-arched doors contributed a simple form of brick ornamentation in tune with the 'economy of labour and therefore great simplicity of design … owing to war-time conditions' (Fig 3.12).

In addition to the trees and green spaces, a hospital, fire station, Co-operative store and temporary church were provided. Further provision for leisure failed to materialise, despite pressure from residents, so this dimension of local life has to be inferred from documentary sources such as the *Mancot Circular*. The chemists left at the end of the war and the buildings found new uses: the fire station, for example, became a garage then a grocery shop. The Deeside Regional Plan of 1923 cited Mancot as a model for future development.

Figure 3.12 An example of a semi-detached house at Mancot Royal, Flintshire, built to house workers at the Queensferry Explosives Works (© Helen Caffrey)

all munitions factories accommodation for key workers, such as the police and foremen, will be found. The influence of pre-war garden city ideals can be seen at sites such as Gretna, but in contrast to other public housing schemes, the factory hierarchy was reflected through the architecture of the estates, in the allocation of detached or semi-detached houses, or in more subtle differences such as the provision of bay windows. In many instances the associated housing remains the most enduring legacy of former factories.

Memorials

During the war around 600 people were killed as a result of accidental explosions in purpose-built munitions works; figures for the loss of life in other types of munitions works are less clear. In places where there was a large loss of life, such as Chilwell, Nottingham; Faversham, Kent; and Silvertown, East London, specially commissioned monuments were built. Elsewhere, memorial plaques and individual graves may be found. The deceased may also be commemorated on their local war memorials – the Leeman Road, York, memorial for example lists people killed in an explosion at Barnbow, Leeds.

3.3 Transport

Railways

In 1914 railways were the dominant form of transport in Britain. The country was covered by a dense network of lines that had been built progressively over the previous 90 years and most towns and many villages had at least one railway station. The system was operated by more than 120 separate railway companies, often competing for traffic over different routes between major centres, but sometimes co-operating to run long-distance trains such as the East Coast Main Line services between London and Scotland that were provided jointly by the Great Northern, North Eastern and North British Railways.

In the years before the start of the First World War it had become apparent to the British government that the railways would play a major role in any future hostilities and that the fragmented ownership and operation of the railway system might lead to delays to military and other essential traffic. Therefore plans were made for state control of the railways in times of war, culminating in the setting up of the Railway Executive Committee in 1912. This Committee, consisting of the General Managers of many of the larger railway companies, assumed control of the railway system on behalf of the government at midnight on 4 August 1914, one hour after war was declared.

As part of mobilisation, there was an immediate need for many special trains to convey troops to the Channel ports, though this was soon exceeded by the continuing requirements for movement of troops and supplies to ports and military bases throughout Britain as the scale of hostilities increased.

Less-obvious impacts on the railways were the loss of large numbers of staff who enlisted for military service, the commandeering of equipment including locomotives, wagons, motor vehicles and horses for use overseas, restrictions on the availability of materials for maintenance and repair work, and the partial turning over of railway workshops to armaments production.

To meet these challenges, the railways sought to discourage unnecessary leisure travel. The various types of cheap tickets were progressively withdrawn and ordinary fares were increased, most restaurant and sleeping cars ceased to operate in 1916, service frequency was reduced on many routes, and some branch lines and intermediate stations were closed altogether for the duration of the war. Despite these measures, non-military passenger traffic continued to rise, probably reflecting increased disposable income of people engaged in war work.

Accidents

The intensity of train operations during the war years was undoubtedly a contributory factor in a number of serious accidents, including the multiple collision and subsequent fire at Quintinshill, near Gretna, in 1915 which remains the worst accident in British railway history. Although the primary cause of the accident was errors made by the signalmen in handling an unusually high number of trains, the exceptional death toll of 227 included 215 men of the 1/7th (Leith) Battalion, Royal Scots who were travelling in a troop train for which old wooden coaches with outdated gas lighting had been pressed into service.

New lines

Even though the railways handled a huge volume of extra wartime traffic, no new main lines were built. There were some new branch lines, for example the Inverness harbour branch which was constructed in as little as two weeks in 1915, involving the laying of three-quarters of a mile of new railway and demolition of two buildings that stood in the way. In addition, a few strategic link lines were built on the instructions of the Railway Executive Committee to provide diversionary routes by connecting previously separate railways. Some of these links survive as important parts of today's railway network, for example the connection between the former Tottenham & Hampstead and London & North Western Railways at Gospel Oak which is now part of the main freight route between Tilbury Docks and the West Coast Main Line, whilst others, such as the link between the Great Northern and Midland Railways at Peterborough, proved to be of little value and were removed at the end of the war.

Most of the main railway companies found it necessary to increase the capacity of key routes by provision of extra running lines or loops, or through signalling alterations. Extra sidings were provided at many locations to serve new factories and military bases or to handle new traffic flows, and platform lengthening took place at several small stations to cater for workers at newly opened factories.

In addition to the works undertaken by the railway companies, some new

Figure 3.13a The train
ferry loading bridge
at Richborough
(Courtesy of
Sandwich Guildhall
Archive)

Figure 3.13b The
bridge was later
relocated to Harwich
(© Catrina Appleby)

facilities were built by the military, most notably at Richborough where 65 miles
of sidings were laid down as part of a new cross-channel port to be used by the
first roll-on / roll-off train ferries; one of the loading bridges was later relocated to
Harwich where it still survives (Fig 3.13 a & b). At Catterick in North Yorkshire,
a dedicated railway system was built to serve the new army camp, and at HM
Factory, Gretna, some 125 miles of track were constructed to move material and
people around the enormous site.

There were also reductions in railway capacity. Some branch lines were
temporarily closed and in the case of the Highland Railway's Buckie branch the

track was lifted and reused to build a new line to the US Navy mine depot at Dalmore, between Alness and the Invergordon naval base from which the mines were taken out to be placed. The construction of the Cromarty branch line was abandoned at the outbreak of war and was never completed, despite the large naval presence in the area. Another well-known example of capacity reduction was the singling of the North Eastern Railway's Whitby and Pickering line (now the North Yorkshire Moors Railway) between Levisham and Pickering to provide rails for use in France.

Memorials

Large numbers of railway staff enlisted for military service and at the end of the war memorials were erected to those who did not return. Generally these took the form of brass plaques at many of the larger stations on the network, such as Edinburgh Waverley, but more elaborate examples include the Victory Arch at Waterloo station, the London and North Western Railway's monument outside Euston station which features four servicemen standing with heads bowed and arms reversed, and the North Eastern Railway's impressive war memorial in York which was designed by Sir Edwin Lutyens.

Traces

Some of the physical evidence of the impact of the First World War on Britain's railways survives in an obvious form. A number of the enhancements to the network are still in use and most war memorials continue to be maintained. However, much has been lost or obscured by subsequent changes. Facilities that were no longer required were often removed at the end of the war, though traces of earthworks may still remain, as at the Barnbow ammunition factory near Leeds. Other facilities were further developed by the railway companies or were modified for reuse in the Second World War. The loss of goods traffic to road transport in the 1950s, the closure of branch lines and intermediate stations following Dr Beeching's *Reshaping of British Railways* report in 1963, and the extensive modernisation of the railways over the last 50 years have all had a major impact on the preservation of First World War remains, though evidence can still be revealed by careful study.

Researching railways at war

The contribution of the railways to Britain's war effort is recorded in Edwin A Pratt's definitive history *British Railways and the Great War*, published in 1921 and based on official records and personal accounts. It is available on the internet courtesy of Cornell University Library. Although this is a lengthy book which deals with organisation and administrative matters in great detail, it cannot cover all the physical changes that took place to the railway system. Fortunately, large numbers of historic railway documents have survived and extensive collections

Supplying the Fleet

Supplying the Royal Navy's Grand Fleet at Scapa Flow presented a particular challenge as the nearest railhead at Thurso could only be reached via the Highland Railway's line from Inverness: 154 miles of single track with infrequent passing places. The military installations at Invergordon, along with some 7000 troops stationed at training camps in the area, only added to the problems. The routes south and east of Inverness were also mostly single lines of low capacity. In view of these limitations, much of the food, ordnance and general supplies for the Fleet was shipped from Aberdeen or Grangemouth. The Highland Railway did, however, manage to transport some of that traffic, together with most of the construction material and subsequent supplies for the naval dockyard at Invergordon and a greatly expanded volume of timber traffic for use as pit props and for military installations. There was also a daily through passenger service between London Euston and Thurso to carry naval personnel: a journey of 717 miles with a planned journey time of around 22 hours. Coal for the Fleet came from south Wales, with trains marshalled at Pontypool Road and dispatched north via Crewe and Carlisle. These trains became known as the 'Jellicoe Specials', named after the Admiral of the Grand Fleet (Fig 3.14). Almost 5½ million tons of coal was moved in this way in the course of the war and there could be up to 100 trains per week. Clearly this was beyond the capacity of the Highland Railway, so most of the coal went to Grangemouth and thence by sea to Scapa Flow.

Figure 3.14 The only known photograph of an Admiralty coal train (a so-called 'Jellicoe Special') is this image of an L&NWR 'B' Class Compound 0-8-0 No. 500 (later LM&S No. 9295 when converted to Class 'G2a') climbing Shap with an unidentified rear banker (© John Alsop Collection)

are held by The National Archives, the National Railway Museum (NRM), Network Rail and various specialist railway societies.

To establish works dating to the First World War on a particular route or at a particular location, a good starting point would be the Minute Books of the relevant railway company, held mainly by The National Archives, as all significant investment would have required approval by the main Board or a sub-committee. The details of the works to be undertaken would be set out in weekly or fortnightly Operating Notices and the end results (such as extra running lines or new signal boxes) would be recorded in the Sectional Appendix to the Working Timetable. (The exact titles of these documents varied between companies.) Operational documents might be found at the NRM or may be held by the Signalling Records Society or a specialist society dedicated to the particular railway company. In some cases the actual engineering drawings for new works might have survived and could be held by the NRM or Network Rail.

Inland waterways

At the outbreak of war, the government immediately foresaw the need to transport huge quantities of troops and munitions as well as the normal freight of the country. Motorised goods transport was still in its infancy and the inland waterways were thought to have had their day so the railways were brought under the immediate control of the government through the Railway Executive Committee. Technically, railway-owned canals came under the same control but in practice were ignored by the government scheme.

The war was a time of soaring inflation, with running costs and some other expenses more than doubling. The railways were protected by the government scheme which guaranteed their net revenues at 1913 levels, thus allowing them to charge uneconomic rates, but inland waterways had no such help and had to face the crippling cost rises alone. In addition, canal and carrying companies suffered serious losses of boat crews as men left to enlist or to go to better-paid work. Boats were also in short supply; some had been sent to the Front, others lay idle for want of repairs. Horses used for hauling barges were also lost to the army.

The decades leading up to the war had seen a slight increase in tonnage carried on the canals but, from 1914, traffic declined dramatically. Traffic on the railways meanwhile had increased and by 1916 they were severely overburdened. In February 1917, in an effort to relieve rail transport, the government took control of the main independent waterways, together with the railway-owned canals. By the summer of 1917, some of the principal carrying companies had also been brought under government control. The scheme meant that financial help and other support could be offered to the operators. A central Canal Control Committee was formed, with four regional committees. The main issues they had to deal with were labour shortages, industrial unrest, and wage claims.

Efforts to recruit civilian men to work on the boats were not very successful. There was some recruitment of women but they worked only on shore-based tasks, mainly loading and unloading. In June 1917, Union resistance to the use

GERMAN
PRISONERS
AT WORK
№ 10.

A.J.HARMSWORTH & SONS
Boat Builders North Camp
ALDERSHOT.

Figure 3.15 German
PoWs unloading
timber at Frimley
Wharf, on the
Basingstoke Canal
in Surrey (Courtesy
of Basingstoke Canal
Society)

of troops to work on canals was overcome and a training school was set up at
Devizes on the Kennet and Avon Canal. Prisoners of war were also put to work
on the canal network (Fig 3.15). Troops from the Transport Battalions were also
trained on the Leeds and Liverpool Canal and the Rochdale Canal. At Devizes,
men underwent a three-week training programme and were then sent to work,
mainly in the Midlands. By September 1918 it was said that around 135 men had
been trained at Devizes; the training scheme was then closed down, having served
its purpose.

While some traffic was transferred from rail to canal during the period,
the inland waterways could do little to relieve the railways. Shortages of boats
and crews, and the neglected state of the canals, meant that they were not in a
position to take much more traffic. One exception, however, was the Caledonian
Canal which saw a large increase in traffic in 1918 shipping American-built sea
mines to the US Navy mine depot at Inverness. There were also problems with
the fragmentary nature of the industry. Through routes would come under the
ownership of several different canal and railway companies making it difficult
to get quotes for long-distance rates of carriage. The multiplicity of ownership
also meant that there was little co-operation over repairing and improving the
waterways. Although exacerbated by wartime conditions, none of this was new
and had long been a demotivating factor to potential senders of traffic.

Canal transport did play a small part in supporting the war effort overseas.
The Inland Water Transport Battalion of the Royal Engineers was set up in 1915
and served in France, Belgium and the Far East. It supplied the Front in France,
helped with evacuations, moved troops and provided hospital boats. Some of

the men drafted into this Battalion were experienced canal workers; others were trained on the Basingstoke Canal which was under the management of the Royal Engineers during the war.

At the end of the war there was some feeling that the inland waterways should be nationalised. However, this did not fit with existing government policy which was against giving further subsidies to any industry. The canals were released from government control at the end of August 1920 although railway control and subsidy continued for another year.

The First World War, and government policy during the period, dealt a severe blow to the canal industry and was probably more significant in bringing about their eventual demise than anything which followed. While few alterations were made to the canal network as a direct consequence of the war, locally they continued to play an important role in the wartime economy. Surviving company records, many of which are held in The Waterways Archive at the National Waterways Museum, Ellesmere Port, may record the goods that they carried.

3.4 Agriculture

On Wednesday 6 August 1914 Walter G Slack, a well-to-do north Shropshire farmer, noted in his diary 'Finished thatching [the ricks]. At mangolds. War declared against Germany.' Probably for Slack, as a farmer, the outbreak of war was good news – remembering past conflicts, especially the Napoleonic Wars of 1795–1815, no doubt he anticipated something of a boom in the few months the war was expected to last, a respite from 40 years of hard times for farmers. Agriculture had been in the doldrums since the 1870s when Britain committed to free trade, bringing in cheap North American wheat and refrigerated meat from the Americas, Australia and New Zealand; by 1900 over half the country's food was imported, and astute observers were already questioning if the country could feed itself during a protracted European war.

How that was managed is one of the most important stories about the First World War. Just how essential agricultural production was to the war effort was fully appreciated by contemporaries, and is well-documented in modern studies, certainly in terms of statistics. Yet very little remains to be seen on the ground today, although of course the farmland that was ploughed up, the town parks that became allotments, and the woods that were clear-felled, often still retain a sense of this history. Thus, perhaps more than any other aspect of the Home Front story, this is one dominated by the historical framework.

The Land

To begin with, although food prices steadily rose, its availability was of little general concern. There were two years of bumper harvests, food imports were little affected, and despite the rush to the colours enough men remained, just, to

Figure 3.16 The Waggoners Memorial at Sledmere, North Yorks, erected by Sir Mark Sykes in memory of the men lost from the Waggoners Reserve. The panels on the monument tell the story of the Waggoners Reserve in the war, including this depiction of a man receiving his call-up papers during the harvest (© Jonathan Finch; Catrina Appleby)

till the land. Locally, however, the impact could be severe. On the eve of war Sir Mark Sykes raised the thousand-strong Waggoners Reserve on the Sledmere estate on the East Yorkshire Wolds to provide skilled waggon drivers for the army (Fig 3.16). Many received their call-up papers in the harvest field, and within a fortnight were operating army transport in northern France. However, in general it was after the call went out for a New Army in September 1914 (Lord Kitchener's famous 'Your Country Needs You' appeal) that the countryside emptied of many of its strong young men, and by the time of the food production campaign of 1917 farming was about 21% short of its labour requirements.

That campaign became necessary because in 1916 a poor harvest was followed by the Kaiser's announcement that he would starve Britain into submission by unrestricted submarine warfare. Merchant shipping losses rose threefold to 875,000 tons a month in April 1917; little food was left in store, and only six weeks' supply of wheat. Official intervention had become essential. The coalition government set up in December 1916 under Lloyd George appointed a Food Controller, and minimum prices to be paid for potatoes and cereals were introduced. The planting of relatively new crops like sugar beet was encouraged, while conversely the exceptional wartime conditions supported traditional crafts and industries which had been waning. In August 1917 the Ministry of Munitions purchased the entire British flax crop to make uniforms, including that of the historic linen trade along the Norfolk/Suffolk border.

Rationing and propaganda

In spite of the country's heavy reliance on food imports in 1914, the government proved very reluctant to attempt to control the food markets during the war. Compulsory rationing was not introduced until late 1917/early 1918, and the first Ration Books didn't appear until 15 July 1918. The government's principal concern was the supply of wheat, which was hit particularly hard by the loss of merchant shipping in the Atlantic, although many other commodities were also in short supply. The wheat shortage was compounded by a world-wide poor harvest in 1916.

Figure 3.17 Cover of the *Win-the-War Cookery Book*

The government-approved *Win-the-War Cookery Book*, with its mixture of propaganda and public information, was published in early 1917 (Fig 3.17). The emphasis was very firmly on reducing wheat consumption; the recipes use large amounts of butter and sugar which by 1918 were also subject to rationing. In the emotive language of propaganda, the book conveys the message that by eating less bread, the country can defeat the U-boats. Its target audience was clearly middle-class women, with references to 'educating one's servants' and the suggestion that the middle class should reduce their bread consumption in order to leave more for the working class for whom it is the staple food. Along with recipes utilising more plentiful foods such as oats, the book places great emphasis on reducing waste. Messages at the bottom of each page include: 'Waste bread and you waste shells' and 'Eat less, masticate more'! An emotive address 'To the Women of Britain' on the first page talks of beating the Germans 'in the larder and the kitchen', and concludes 'Will you fail the children?'

Other measures included the granting of enhanced powers to County Agricultural Executive Committees (established in 1915) to order grassland to be ploughed up and even to take over poorly run farms; the formation of a Labour Corps in January 1917 to bring elderly, unfit or wounded soldiers, eventually numbering 175,00 across the UK as a whole, onto the land; the creation of the Women's Land Army (preceded by the Women's Land Service Corps) (Fig 3.18) in February 1917 which eventually reached a strength of 16,000 women, mainly drawn from the middle class; the release of skilled farmworkers from the Front on furlough to help with ploughing and the harvest, using horses hired from army camps; and the employment of 30,000 PoWs in farm work. In East Anglia, at least, extensive use was also made on the land of schoolboys aged twelve and over, their farmer-employers being granted school exemption certificates.

Figure 3.18 Women's Land Army recruitment poster

For *Country Life* agricultural machinery was 'the ammunition of the land army', and its vital role needs to be understood. Petrol-engined tractors had been available since the 1890s, and 900 three-wheeler Ivels were made in England between 1902 and 1914. However, in all there are unlikely to have been more than 1000 tractors in the UK at the outbreak of war. The much greater numbers required to raise wartime production, especially from 1916, meant government purchasing agencies looked to the United States, and the 15,000 tractors imported in 1917 introduced new brand names to the farm: the Moghul, Titan, Overtime, and Moline. In addition, 6000 Fordsons were ordered, even though it remained in prototype; when they arrived (far from all before the war's end though) they proved both reliable and popular. Almost 10,000 ploughs were also bought in.

Overall, in 1917 and especially 1918, roughly a million acres of grassland in Britain were ploughed up to grow crops, and in the Tamar Valley and elsewhere 18th- and 19th-century lime kilns came back into production, for a final time, to burn lime to sweeten or neutralise newly ploughed acid soils. Largely because of these measures, even though rationing had to be introduced in late 1917, starvation was avoided.

Physical evidence of the ploughing-up campaign, most extensive in west and north England, and Wales, is probably lost. At the end of the war the new arable typically went back to grass, and then was ploughed up again in the Second World War when five times as much land went under the plough than it had 25 years before.

Forestry

There was a growing feeling from the late 19th century that a national forestry policy was needed, but nothing had been done by 1914: at that time only five percent of Britain was wooded – the lowest percentage since the Middle Ages – and 90 percent of the country's wood supplies were imported. Yet, once the war started, there was an almost insatiable demand from the Western Front for timber and wood for all manner of construction work, from camps to duckboards. At least as important were the pit props needed in Britain's mines as without coal, industry could not be powered or the Fleet kept under steam. As with food, the problems became acute in 1916 and the Acland Committee was set up to look into woodland production, although it was not until 1919 that the Forestry Commission was established.

The Horse

The army's almost insatiable demand for horses (and mules) for transport and artillery hauling – animals coped better than lorries in the mud of Flanders – saw the establishment of specialist remount depots where the animals were gathered in and trained for their new roles. Initially mobilisation saw horses drawn from the land, and as this was thought to be a war where cavalry would play a vital role, from the stables of country houses and hunts: 'How many will ever again hear the sound of the horn?', plaintively asked *Country Life*. In fact, most of the 467,000 horses later bought in the UK probably came from towns and industry. While this meant that the number of farm horses fell by only a few percent between 1914 and 1916, there were too few to match the requirements of the ploughing-up campaign. But wherever they were drawn from (over 400,000 horses were also purchased abroad), the army's horses required feeding: again new systems had to be set up to gather fodder and to ship it to Flanders. In March 1917, 70,000 tons of hay per month were being shipped across the Channel and in bulk terms more fodder was taken to France than munitions. For a firm of rope-makers in Bridport (Somerset) it brought a massive boost in business: a million hay-nets were supplied for the wartime army.

Remount depots for gathering and training horses and mules were run by the Army Service Corps. One such depot had already been set up in 1891 at Woolwich, London, and a futher one in Lusk, just north of Dublin, prior to the Boer War. These depots were retained and two more sites were added at Melton

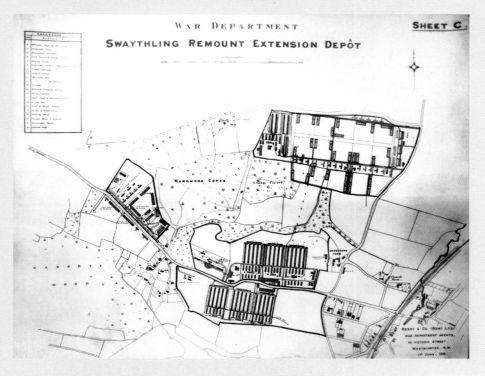

Figure 3.19 Plan of the Swaythling Remount Depot (© TNA)

Mowbray, Leicestershire, and Arborfield Cross, Berkshire. The new depots were termed 'remount farms' and comprised a few stables and agricultural buildings along with grazing land where the horses could be kept. However, it soon became evident that the scale of horse mobilisation in the event of a European war had been underestimated and from 1914 to 1915 further large reception remount depots were set up to receive imported horses at Ormskirk, to serve Liverpool docks, and Shirehampton for receiving animals arriving by sea at Avonmouth. Two more large depots were established: Romsey, in Hampshire, was primarily a training and conditioning depot, while Swaythling, near Southampton, was responsible for collecting horses from Reserve units and training depots and forwarding them on to France (Fig 3.19).

The impact of remount mobilisation was evident across Great Britain. The remount centres at Romsey, Swaythling, and Arborfield were vast and would have been imposing features in the landscape, although the physical remains of these sites today are limited. The Infirmary stables of 1911–12 at Arborfield do survive and are a scheduled monument (Fig 3.20). Records suggest that there must have been numerous collecting depots to handle the large number of animals impressed, but these centres were ephemeral, set up as and when they were required, and even the larger depots were built for short-term use, many being abandoned rapidly after demobilisation.

As on the land in general, men left the country's woods and forests to serve in the forces, notwithstanding the increased demand for what they produced. Nor were the country's sawmills able to meet demand. In response, a new labour force entered the woods including PoWs, the Canadian Forestry Corps (CFC) whose several thousand members included many based at Windsor Great Park, some 400 American lumberjacks operating in northern Scotland, and the 2000-strong Women's Forestry Corps created in 1917 as a separate body from the Women's Land Army. So acute was the need for timber and wood, not least to maximise the amount of food ships could bring to Britain, that ancient woods, parkland trees and ornamental avenues all fell to axe and saw, as did hedgerow trees: in 1923 a visitor commented how depressing it was to see the Wolds around Sledmere so denuded of trees by the necessity of wartime. The large forestry camps set up by Canadians in Rothiemurchus Forest, near Aviemore, have left little trace apart from the concrete base of the sawmill and the tramway systems used to haul trees to the mill. Stanton Moor in Derbyshire, which by the early 19th century was almost entirely planted with fir, larch, oak and Spanish chestnut, was clear-felled towards the end of the war using local female labour under the supervision of a CFC unit. The timber was extracted to a temporary sawmill using an animal-hauled narrow-gauge light railway, earthwork traces of which still remain. In all, it is estimated that 450,000 acres of woodland were felled in Britain.

'Allotmentitis'

As food shortages mounted, ever-more official encouragement was given to 'growing your own'. From December 1916 local authorities were empowered to create allotments, and municipal parks, school playing fields, golf courses and waste land were all given over to vegetable growing. 'Allotmentitis' swept the country, and by 1918 the number of allotments had grown threefold since 1914 to c 1.5 million growing 2 million tons of vegetables a year. While parks and playing fields returned to recreational use once the war ended, the number of allotments overall remained at roughly twice the 1914 number during the inter-war years.

3.5 Dissent and conscientious objection

Between the introduction of conscription in 1916 and the end of the war more than 20,000 British men refused to fight for 'King and Country'. For a small hard core of maybe 1400 this meant imprisonment until 1919; for others, about 4000, it meant imprisonment before release to a Home Office Work Centre. For a further 5000 it meant various forms of non-combatant service under army control or in the Friends Ambulance Unit. The remainder, about half of the total, were deemed to be in war-essential work and were excused military service or were directed to work of national importance in industry or on the land.

Documentary evidence to tell the story of these Conscientious Objectors is patchy. Indeed, during the war and for many years afterwards the very fact of their existence was barely acknowledged and subjected to a process of determined forgetting. At a stroke, with the destruction of local Tribunal records in 1922, notwithstanding certain selected and other random survivals, the official documentary history of Britain's Conscientious Objectors was almost wiped out. Nevertheless, that difficulty is now being resolved. The *Pearce Register of British Conscientious Objectors*, online with the Imperial War Museum's 'Lives of the First World War' platform, has begun to detail the individual stories of more than 17,000 Conscientious Objectors.

Where physical evidence for Conscientious Objectors is concerned the picture is far from clear. Some key physical indicators do remain although are seldom identified as such. For example, most of the prisons where they were held are still with us. Of the four prisons cleared for use as Conscientious Objector

Figure 3.21 The recently rediscovered Conscientious Objectors memorial rock at Greenmoor

Work Centres between 1916 and 1919, Warwick and Knutsford have both been demolished, but Dartmoor and Wakefield still survive. Yet, with the exception of the Conscientious Objectors' graffiti which English Heritage has preserved at Richmond Castle, along with items in the Dartmoor Prison Museum, little else that remains has been identified as being related to Conscientious Objectors. However, new evidence is still coming to light: histories of Socialist Conscientious Objectors had, for many years, described a rock in the Lake District close to a 'safe house' for Conscientious Objectors on the run. On the rock, it was said, men who had used the safe house carved their initials (Fig 3.21). The house (farmhouse) is called 'Greenmoor' and is at Woodlands, near Broughton in Furness in the southern Lake District. A team of Lake District Archaeology Volunteers have recently discovered the rock, some two hundred metres from the house (Fig 3.22). The initials carved in it are those of men with connections to Halifax in West Yorkshire. Chief among them are those of members of the Stoker family. William Richard Stoker was a well-to-do draper from Halifax whose own house was called 'Greenmore'. He and his brothers, Tom and Harry, were members of a radical Socialist group known as the Socialist Labour Party.

The only formal memorial to the First World War's Conscientious Objectors is in Tavistock Square gardens in London. Promoted by the Peace Pledge Union, it was unveiled for the first time in 1994 by Sir Michael Tippett, a Second World War Conscientious Objector.

Figure 3.22 View from the memorial rock to the 'safe house' Greenmoor

Public Open Spaces

The enormous proliferation of army depots and barracks across the country created pressure on local public open spaces for use as drill grounds and for recruits' basic training. This was particularly true of Birkenhead. The local barracks was a depot for the Cheshire Regiment and Birkenhead Park was used for basic training. As a public open space it attracted spectators, and in the autumn of 1916 it was the site of a notorious case of army brutality. In an attempt to persuade a group of Conscientious Objectors to give in NCOs, under orders from their Commanding Officer, man-handled and abused Conscientious Objectors around the Park's assault course, throwing them over barriers and into ditches, and rolling them down embankments. The Conscientious Objectors remained determined but members of the public were outraged. There was an enquiry and the practice stopped.

Roads

The Home Office Scheme for Conscientious Objectors was introduced in August 1916. It arose from concerns expressed by the army and by Asquith's Liberal government that Conscientious Objectors who had served their first sentences had no other option but to be returned to their army units to face another court martial and another prison sentence. This not only took up a great deal of army time – about a third of all courts martial in the summer of 1916 involved Conscientious Objectors – but also carried the political risk of a great many imprisoned Conscientious Objectors becoming 'martyrs' who would bring the conscription system, not to mention the war as a whole, into disrepute. A Parliamentary Committee chaired by William Brace, Under-Secretary of State at the Home Office, was created in an attempt to deal with this. What they came up with was a scheme of public works which were not thought to be war-related and which, therefore, might be acceptable as useful employment for Conscientious Objectors. Initially these were road works under the auspices of the Ministry of Transport and local Road Boards. The Conscientious Objectors lived on site in existing buildings, tents or huts. There were many small schemes but thoses employing larger numbers included:

> Suffolk Road Board Scheme – employed 50 Conscientious Objectors making roads at Clare, Haverhill and Kedington from August 1916.

> Dyce Quarry, Aberdeen – established August 1916 to quarry road stone for local road repairs and construction. Poorly managed, with more than 250 Conscientious Objectors living under leaky canvas. One Conscientious Objector died of pneumonia and the camp was closed after two months.

Figure 3.23 A painting
of the camp at
Caolas-na-con, near
Kinlochleven, by a
German PoW
(© RCAHMS)

Denton Road Board Camp, Newhaven, East Sussex – established
by November 1916 and employed over 150 Conscientious Objectors,
making and repairing roads in and around Newhaven.

Ballachulish, Argyll County Road Board – a scheme to
construct a new road on the southern shore of Loch Leven to the
aluminium smelter at Kinlochleven. There was a camp for the
Conscientious Objectors at Caolas-na-Con near Kinlochleven
(Fig 3.23). Begun in October 1916, it eventually employed more
than 240 Conscientious Objectors. Their place was taken after
July 1917 by PoWs.

Dartmoor landscape reclamation

By the end of February 1917, the last of Dartmoor prison's 300 criminal inmates
had been moved out and distributed to other prisons. Within a short time it
became home to 1200 Conscientious Objectors. In addition to work necessary
for the prison's inmates, on its farm and in its quarry, Conscientious Objectors
were also involved with a scheme of landscape reclamation on the estate of the
Duchy of Cornwall.

The scheme, known as the Tor Royal or Tor Park newtake, involved reclaiming
1200 acres (c 486ha) of granite-strewn moorland according to a plan drawn up by
the Belgian agricultural engineer, Henry Vendelman (Fig 3.24).

Figure 3.24 A Conscientious Objectors work party at Tor Royal on Dartmoor (Courtesy of Cyril Pearce)

Tor Royal Party.

Figure 3.25 Huts used to house Conscientious Objectors employed by Llanelli Rural District Council in building a reservoir and water treatment works at Llanddeusant, near Llandovery (Courtesy of Cyril Pearce)

Waterworks and reservoirs

In a statement to the House of Commons on 17 October 1916, William Brace announced that 118 Conscientious Objectors were employed on the repair and construction of waterworks under the Llanelli Rural District Council at Llanon and at Llanddeusant, near Llandovery. Some of the men were lodged in a local farmhouse, the others in huts (Fig 3.25).

Sunk Island, Patrington, near Hull

Beyond the civil engineering projects, Conscientious Objectors were also involved in more obviously humanitarian work. By April 1917 about 36 of them were helping to build a farm colony for discharged, and presumably disabled, soldiers on the Crown estate at Sunk Island.

Coast and sea

4.1 Introduction

Through necessity, being a maritime nation, Britain has always looked to the sea as a means of transport, trade and defence, with the Royal Navy protecting our shores and overseas trade, while the army would defend against an invasion. In August 1914 Britain's shores were defended by a legacy of powerful Victorian forts, many of which had recently been modernised and supplemented by quick-firing batteries to meet the threat of smaller and fast-moving torpedo boats. Technological advances during the thirty years preceding the outbreak of the First World War ensured a revolution in the capabilities of both the Royal Navy and the army (which was responsible for the Coast Defence batteries). The period witnessed the introduction of breech-loading (BL) and quick-firing (QF) artillery which could fire high-explosive and armour-piercing shells; Dreadnought battleships and battlecruisers driven by steam turbines; range-finding and plotting instruments allowing accurate fire beyond the horizon; telephone and wireless communication; bolt-action magazine-rifles; machine-guns; and airships and aeroplanes.

Figure 4.1 Milford Haven Port War Signal Station (Courtesy of R J C Thomas)

The signing of the Entente Cordiale between Britain and France in 1904 (and later treaties with Russia), and the recognition of Imperial Germany's militarism and aggressive foreign policy, led to a rapid expansion of the Royal Navy and a gradual shift in the emphasis of defences from the south to the east coast of the British Isles. In addition to the existing naval bases, originally built to operate against the French navy, new ones were established at Harwich, the Humber, the Tyne, Blyth, Rosyth, Invergordon (Cromarty Firth), Scapa Flow, and Shetland. New low-profile mass-concrete gun emplacements armed with 9.2-inch BL, 6-inch BL, 4.7-inch QF, and 12-pounder QF guns were built to protect the approaches to the Royal Dockyards and other ports and

Figure 4.2 Bull Sand
Fort, off Spurn Point,
River Humber
(© English Heritage)

harbours that were considered vulnerable to attack. These artillery defences were supplemented by Port War Signal Stations (Fig 4.1), anti-submarine and anti-destroyer boom defences, magnetic submarine detection loops (from 1917), Royal Engineer Submarine Mining Establishments, hydrophone stations, blockships, anti-submarine hurdles, anti-torpedo nets, coast-watching observation posts, and naval 'Y Station' radio interception posts.

As the war progressed, these defences were further enhanced by the construction of additional forts and batteries, including two sea forts and two 9.2-inch gun batteries to defend the Humber (Fig 4.2), a pair of 12-inch gun turrets landed from the pre-Dreadnought battleship HMS *Illustrious* to defend the Tyne, many new 6-inch and smaller batteries at Scapa Flow and on the Forth, and numerous Royal Navy Air Stations, operating both fixed-wing aircraft and airships, with no fewer than eight sited around Scapa Flow alone. During the course of the war the number of guns protecting the fleet anchorage and naval base at Rosyth, the greatest fortress in Scotland, rose from 12 to 44.

In addition to the changes taking place in the defences, new but less glamorous facilities were also being built within the naval bases for the operation of mine-layers, submarines, and the oil-fired warships. Coal wharfs were gradually being replaced by oil depots with extensive tank farms and jetties, such as that at Invergordon where 40 original oil tanks survive. The use of aircraft and airships by both the German army and navy ensured that passive air defence became an aspect of the design of these facilities and that they were provided with anti-aircraft defences. The massive growth in the manpower necessary to operate the fleet, the artillery defences, and the various ancillary services led to the construction of vast numbers of temporary hutments. Many of these were dismantled and offered for sale in the early 1920s, finding new uses as homes, village halls, reading rooms and club houses.

4.2 Coastal defences

Coast artillery defences had guarded harbours, ports, and beaches in England ever since the reign of Henry VIII. A well-chosen strategic location from the Tudor period, like Pendennis Castle, Falmouth, was re-fortified on several occasions down the centuries. Many of the fortifications were altered and added to in a piecemeal fashion and it was not until the Royal Commission on the Defences of the United Kingdom made their report in 1860 that any attempt was made to ensure a degree of standardisation. Until the end of the 19th century France and Russia remained the principal bogeymen for contemporary invasion scare stories, but by the turn of the century their place had been taken by Germany, a shift most well-known through Erskine Childers' novel *The Riddle of the Sands*, that told the story of a plot to invade eastern England from the German Frisian Islands.

The rapid technological advances of the latter half of the 19th century and the haphazard introduction of these new developments meant that by the end of the 19th century there was a chaotic variety of obsolete guns and fortifications – a veritable Quartermaster's nightmare. Work commenced in the late 1890s to rectify the situation, with the introduction of new breech-loading and quick-firing guns, mounted in new low-profile mass-concrete gun emplacements, served by underground magazines.

The majority of these new gun emplacements were built during the first decade of the 20th century to defend dockyards, ports and harbours at Portsmouth, Plymouth, Dover, Portland, Falmouth, the Severn estuary, Thames & Medway, Mersey, Tees, Tyne, Milford Haven, Kingston upon Hull (Paull Point),

Figure 4.3 Remains of the Sunk Island Battery 6" gun tower, River Humber (© R J C Thomas)

Figure 4.4 Hoxa Head 4-inch coast battery, South Ronaldsay (© RCAHMS)

Isles of Scilly, Clyde and Firth of Forth. Many of the new gun batteries were built close to pre-existing fortifications, or even on top of them, as at Garrison Point Fort, Sheerness and Inchkeith Island in the Firth of Forth. Initially these new defences were built to bring Britain's existing defences up to date, but by the beginning of the second decade, the growing threat posed by the Imperial German Navy had been recognised and new plans were rapidly drawn up to provide additional defences for the East Coast ports and especially those on the Humber, where new 6-inch gun batteries at Sunk Island and Stallingborough were under construction at the time the First World War broke out (Fig 4.3). This shift in strategic necessity saw further coast artillery batteries being built on the Humber, Tyne, Forth, Blyth, Cromarty, Shetland, and particularly at Scapa Flow (Fig 4.4). The mouth of the Humber provides a good example of a range of fortifications, many modified for later military purposes or alternative use, such as the RNLI building at Spurn Point (Fig 4.5) which was originally the Royal Artillery Store where spare parts, tools and the delicate parts of the gun were kept. Plans such as this one from The National Archives provide vital information on the layout of the batteries (Fig 4.6).

As in mainland Britain, the early decades of the 20th century saw coastal defences constructed at a number of locations in Ireland. On Belfast Lough, these took the form of two fortifications – Grey Point Fort on the south shore,

Figure 4.5 An RNLI building at Spurn Point which was formerly a Royal Artillery Store (© R J C Thomas)

near Holywood, and Kilroot Battery on the north shore, near Carrickfergus. Construction work began at Grey Point in 1904 with the fort becoming operational by 1907, when the two 6-inch Mark VII breech-loading guns (by Vickers Sons & Maxim Ltd) were first mounted. Associated outbuildings, workshops and stores facilities were progressively erected in the following two to three years.

In 1914 mobilisation for war necessitated further accommodation at the battery in the form of Armstrong hutting. Historical records from the 13th Battalion of the Royal Irish Rifles indicate that recruits from Kitchener's New Army (36th Division) were training in the use of machine-guns and artillery at the fort at this time. While the artillery at the fort was never used in anger during the First World War, it nonetheless provided a successful deterrent against German U-Boats and warships. The defence battery remained in operation after the war as part of the permanent coastal defence of Belfast. Grey Point has been reconstructed and is open to the public.

Construction at Kilroot Battery began in 1910 with the establishment of two east-facing 6-inch Mark VII gun emplacements along with the associated magazine, shell store and shelter which were constructed underneath. The fort layout at Kilroot was diamond-shaped rather than pentagonal and surrounded

Figure 4.6 Plan of battery at Spurn Point. Such plans provide an invaluable guide when searching for physical remains (© TNA)

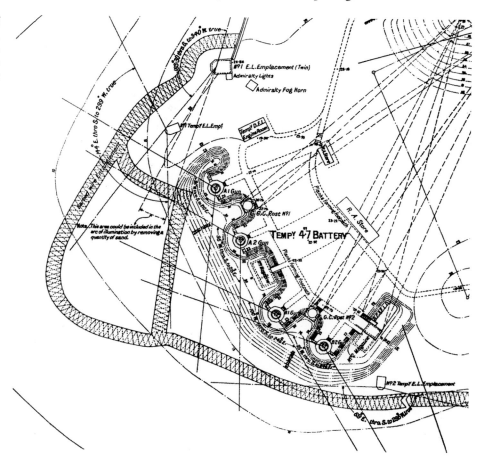

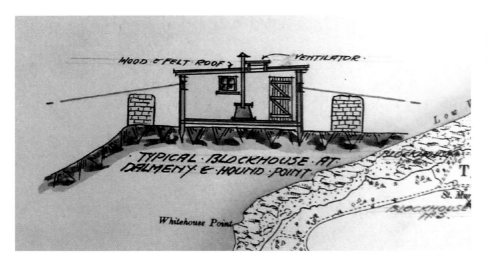

by a defence wall. By 1914 the battery was surrounded by trenches and barbed-wire fencing, creating an 'unclimbable' palisade, further boosted by two lookout posts at the water's edge, armed with machine-guns guarding against an enemy approach from the Irish Sea. Kilroot was further augmented by the installation of two large blockhouses capable of housing approximately eighteen men which were an integral feature in the defence of the fort. Kilroot was decommissioned in 1957. Carrickfergus Castle undertook a number of roles during the war; it was mounted with anti-submarine guns and became part of the Coast Defence Battery of Ireland.

The scale of the defences placed at any particular location varied according to the importance of the harbour and/or the possible scale of an anticipated attack; however, the minimum at all locations would have been a signalling station, a battery observation post, gun emplacements, defence electric lights (DEL) [searchlights], engine houses (to provide power for the lights and guns), and accommodation. A defended naval base or an important port would have had a fortress system of defence, with the Royal Navy manning patrol and inspection craft, boom defence and torpedo nets, wireless signal stations, hydrophone and magnetic loop systems, port control and the Port War Signal Station, which was responsible for identifying all approaching warships. The Royal Garrison Artillery usually manned the long-, medium- and close-range coast artillery (although the Royal Marines manned the guns at bases such as Invergordon), together with the Fire Command Post, Battery Observation Posts and plotting rooms; Royal Engineers manned the telephone communication systems, DEL and engine rooms, while infantrymen manned the landward defences. Prior to the war the coast defence batteries were manned by Territorial batteries of the Royal Garrison Artillery, a role they continued to fulfil for much of the war. The conduct of operations for these defences was laid down in a number of manuals issued to each fortress, including the *Organisation and Fighting of the Coast Armaments* 1911, *Defence Schemes, Fighting Books, Fortress Record Books*, and the *Manual of Coast Fortress Defence* 1914; some of these are available for inspection at The National Archives, Kew.

Gun batteries were often situated to either side of the entrance to the channel leading to a port and in some cases on islands in the middle of an estuary or harbour. In the case of the Humber, two steel fortifications – Bull Sand and Haile Sand Forts – were built on shallow shoals on the river bed (see Fig 4.2). The largest guns installed to defend any port in Britain in the First World War were the ex-naval 12-inch gun turrets installed on either side of the mouth of the Tyne at Marsden (Kitchener Battery) and Hartley (Roberts Battery), although they were not fully operational until 1921 and were dismantled in 1926.

In contrast to the army-built defences, the coast batteries for the Cromarty Firth and the Invergordon Naval Base were built and manned by the navy, using unique designs.

Hexagonal blockhouses were constructed as Coast Defence batteries around mainland Britain and Ireland, fortifying and defending against any possible German attack by land (Fig 4.7). Excellent examples of these can still be seen in Ireland at Grey Point Fort, Belfast Lough; Lenan Head Fort, Lough Swilly; and Fort Dunree, Co Donegal, as well as at Inchkeith Island, Kinghorn and Braefoot Point on the Forth and at Blyth, Northumberland (Fig 4.8). In addition to the blockhouses vast lines of barbed-wire entanglements were positioned and trenches dug affording further fortification. A range of defences still survives on the hills around the Portkil Battery on the Clyde, including the earthwork remains of timber blockhouses and supporting trenches which can be matched with War Office plans and recent aerial photographs. At the Cromarty Firth, two surviving pillboxes of unusual design may be part of the close defence of the North Sutor battery.

Figure 4.8 A restored blockhouse at Blyth, Northumberland (© R J C Thomas)

Coastal defence armament

Subsequent to a decision taken by the Owen Committee of 1906, which was set up to report on British coastal defence, the British army had four types of artillery in place for coastal defence:

9.2-inch BL (breech-loading) Gun Mark X
Carriage Garrison Barbette Mark V allowing 15° elevation
Max Range – 17,400 yards (c 15,900m)
Standard Projectile – Armour Piercing weighing 380 lbs 9.2-inch BL Mark X
Role – long-range counter bombardment of battleships and heavy cruisers

6-inch BL Gun Mark VII
Carriage Garrison CP Mark II allowing 16° elevation
Max Range – 12,600 yards (c 11,500m)
Standard Projectiles – Armour Piercing weighing 100 lbs
Role – to counter light cruisers at medium range

4.7-inch QF (quick-firing) Mark V
Carriage Garrison Mark CP Mark V allowing 20° elevation
Max Range – 16,500 yards (c 15,100m)
Standard Projectile – Common Pointed weighing 45 lbs
Role – to counter light cruisers, armed merchant cruisers, block-ships, and transports

12-Pr 12 cwt QF
Carriage Garrison Mark II allowing 20° elevation
Range – 8000 yards (c 7300m)
Standard Projectiles – Common Pointed weighing 12 lbs 8 oz
Role – to counter fast torpedo boats and torpedo-boat destroyers

In addition to the standard types some obsolescent weapons remained in service and as the war progressed, improvisation also occurred, resulting in a number of other gun types being used. These included the 4-inch QF Marks III and V, the 6-inch QF Mark II, the 7.5-inch Mark I howitzer (naval), the 7.5-inch BL Mark II, the 10-inch BL Mark III, the 12-inch Mark I and the 12-inch Mark VIII

4-inch QF Mark V
Carriage Garrison Mark V
Max Range – 9000 yards (c 8200m)
Standard Projectile – Common Pointed weighing 31 lbs

12-inch BL Gun Mark VIII
Mounting BL 12-inch Mark VIII gun Mark I [Naval mounting B.II]
Max Range – 26,000 yards (c 23,800m) at 30° elevation
Standard Projectile – Armour Piercing weighing 850 lbs

3-Pr QF, 6-Pr QF, 4-inch BL Vavasseur and 5-inch BL Vavasseur were retained in practice batteries alongside of the newer guns

Gun emplacements

All of the new gun emplacements were built to a basic 'standard' design, using mass-concrete construction, with the minimum of reinforcement; the plan was adaptable to suit any given site. The basic structure of the emplacement was a drum of concrete cast around the steel gun holdfast frame and plate. The holdfast plate and bolts were carefully levelled to ensure that the gun, when mounted, was perfectly level. Most emplacements were semi-circular or D-plan in shape, with the curve formed by a concrete apron sloping forward at an angle of 7° fronted by a turf-covered, sand-filled shell deflection apron.

12-Pr and 4.7-inch QF gun emplacements

The 12-Pr and 4.7-inch QF gun emplacements were generally quite simple, with ammunition lockers set into the sides of the structure and below the gun floor, and the magazine and gun store set to each side, either buried into a sloping rampart, or built underground and accessed by a stairway to an open service area at the rear (Fig 4.9). Quick-firing (QF) guns normally used a brass cartridge case to contain the cordite charge with the shell physically attached to the cartridge

Figure 4.9 12-Pr QF gun with breech open at Chapel Bay Fort, Milford Haven (Daphne Russell Collection: courtesy of R J C Thomas)

case. This arrangement means the cartridge is easily handled, relatively safe to store, and is unlikely to be accidentally ignited; consequently the magazine was either a simple single chamber or a single chamber divided into a shell and cartridge store. Both the 12-Pr and 4.7-inch QF coast guns used 'separate-loading' meaning that the shell was not attached to the brass cartridge case and had to be loaded separately.

6-inch and 9.2-inch BL gun emplacements

The 6-inch and 9.2-inch BL gun emplacements were built to considerably more substantial and complex designs, usually in pairs with underground shell and cartridge stores, lamp rooms, gun stores and detachment shelters set in the space between them, accessed by stairways leading to an open service area, which also acted as a light well. The 6-inch gun emplacement consisted of a central circular pit within which stood the gun pedestal (Fig 4.10). The pit was enclosed by a raised semi-circular gun floor accessed by a flight of concrete steps to the rear. Breech-loading (BL) guns always use a separately loaded shell and a silk

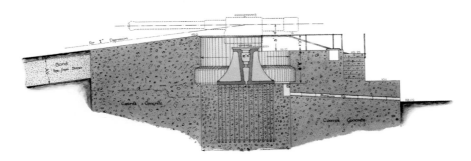

— SECTION D-D —

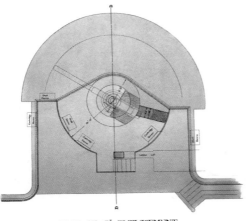

PLAN OF 6" EMPLACEMENT

Figure 4.10 Plan and cross-section of a 6" gun emplacement at Lavernock, south Wales. This is an example of the high-quality plans and drawings available at The National Archives (© TNA)

Figure 4.11 Capt Young, with 9.2" shells and cartridge cylinders (Courtesy of R J C Thomas)

Shalloon bag cartridge, which require special handling to avoid the risk of accidental detonation (Fig 4.11). Consequently the cartridges and shells were always kept separately, with cartridge and shell lockers set into the rear of the gun floor to either side of the steps and the side walls of the emplacement. Although the size of the lockers is the same, they differed in the type of door and frame used. Cartridge lockers were of timber to avoid the risk of a spark, whereas shell locker doors and frames were of steel.

The service floor to the rear of the lockers allowed the ammunition party to operate under the cover of the parapet. A steel hatch in the rear of the gun floor covered a shell hoist that rose at an incline from the magazine below, and a square steel hatch located in the parapet wall or in one of the side walls gave access to the vertical cartridge hoist rising from the magazine.

The magazine consisted of a large rectangular underground structure sub-divided into a number of rooms, served by two corridors with timber shell benches supported on tubular steel frames that acted as the shell stores. A dog-leg at the furthest end of the corridor housed the hand-cranked cartridge and shell hoists. Openings in the walls above the shell benches functioned as lamp recesses for the magazine lamps, which illuminated the magazine. The interior face of the recess, facing into the cartridge stores, had thick glass windows that were protected by zinc or brass wire frames that prevented them from being broken accidentally. During the First World War most magazines were lit by either a tallow candle or a paraffin lamp with a large brass reflector, although a few were lit by electric magazine bulkhead lamps.

To gain access into the cartridge store, a gunner entered through a central 'shifting lobby' from the shell store corridor. The lobby was closed at both ends by double doors, with a timber bench and coat-hooks situated against one wall. The lobby was divided into two halves by a hinged timber barrier and on entering, the gunner had to empty out all of his pockets to ensure no combustible materials were brought into the magazine. He would then have to remove his boots and uniform to reduce the risk of carrying in any grit that might cause a spark, before putting on soft woollen magazine clothing and slippers. The barrier would then have been lifted and he would have been permitted to enter the cartridge store. On coming out, the reverse process took place.

The gun store, usually situated at one end of the open service area, was where tools and the delicate parts of the gun were kept. This was often close to the lamp room, where the magazine lamps were stored. The 'War Shelter', where the duty gun detachment spent their time while on duty, was usually situated in the rear of the open service area, or within the rampart between the two gun emplacements. The War Shelter was often divided into two rooms: the larger men's room was fitted with a pot-bellied stove, timber coat pegs, rifle racks, and a galvanized zinc ventilator, while the officer occupied the smaller and sometimes un-heated room.

The 9.2-inch gun emplacement was altogether larger than that of the 6-inch gun. It comprised three-quarters of a circle with a 'bell-plan' pit (with the exception of Green and Godwin Batteries that were circular) in which stood the gun mounting, bolted to a double ring of off-set holdfast bolts. A recessed duct in the floor carried hydraulic pipes for operating the shell hoist situated in a narrow pit in the floor at the front of the pit. A further hydraulic shell hoist was also attached to the gun mounting. Hydraulic pressure was obtained by using an accumulator situated in a recessed pit at the rear of one side of the emplacement. If the gun had not been fired for some time, the accumulator had to be pumped manually. However, once the gun fired, hydraulic pressure was automatically drawn off from the recoil recuperator on the gun mounting. On the opposite side of the emplacement, a double timber door gave access to the top of an ammunition hoist from the magazine. A number of large cartridge recesses were set into the side walls of the emplacement and a curved shell recess ran around the front of the pit. Two smaller recesses set higher in the side wall were for the gun dials for target information and for fuses and tubes.

A steel gun floor was raised 7ft 2in (2.28m) up above the floor of the gun pit. This consisted of a rotating circular steel platform attached to the gun mounting, with a fixed steel working platform to the rear that was supported on tubular steel stanchions. When the guns were dismantled and taken away, the working platforms were usually scrapped as well, leaving only cut-off stubs in the walls and the steel sockets for stanchions in the floor of the pit.

Ancillary structures

Observation posts come with a number of names, types, functions and designs. These include Fire Command Post (FCP), Port War Signal Station (PWSS), Battery Observation Post (BOP), Battery Command Station (BCS), Battery Command Post (BCP), Position Finding Cell (PF), searchlight Directing Stations (DS), Minefield Observation Posts, and Coast Watcher's Post, some of which could be combined in the same structure. The most basic was the Battery Command Post (BCP), a small, open, semi-circular concrete or timber platform, sufficient for two or three men, with a central concrete Depression Range Finder (DRF) pillar. Battery Observation Posts, PF Cells, and Minefield Observation Posts were often equipped with a Depression Range Finder, which

Figure 4.12 Traces of camouflage paint surviving on the exterior wall at the entrance to the 4-inch QF magazine on the South Sutor at Cromarty (© Allan Kilpatrick)

was mounted on three concrete pillars, or on corbels projecting from the wall. Most were rectangular-plan concrete structures with flat cantilevered roofs over wide observation windows. The large examples were often two storeys high with rest rooms and telephone exchange rooms in the lower floor. In a rare survival, the BOP at South Sutor still has some original navy camouflage paint on an exterior wall, and at the entrance to the 4-inch QF magazine (Fig 4.12).

Communication was usually by field telephone and a recess for the phone can often be found in the wall of the observation post, or in the DRF pillar itself. At the naval site at Cromarty, however, voicepipes were used.

Defence Electric Light (DEL) Emplacements come in a multiplicity of designs. They are usually sub-rectangular in plan, with a large multi-faceted or semi-circular opening at one end facing out to sea. Cable ducts in the floor lead to where the searchlight stood with a circular ventilation hole directly above in the roof to draw off the heat generated by the lamp.

Generator or engine rooms are usually rectangular in plan and often semi-buried. The floor has a number of rectangular mounting blocks for engines, dynamos, and/or generator sets, and the rooms are well ventilated. The floor usually has recessed cable ducts. Diesel oil fuel was stored in tanks outside, sometimes on the surface in walled bunds, or underground.

Test Huts are small, single-storey, brick or concrete cubicles, with a door in the rear wall and no windows, situated to the rear of the battery, or sometimes in hedgelines some distance to the rear. Ventilator bricks can be found close to the floor and under the eaves of the flat concrete roof, and cable ducts for the telephone cables enter through the floor.

Camps were built close to, but to the rear of most coast artillery batteries (Fig 4.13). They included caretaker's or master gunner's cottages, guard rooms,

living huts, canteens, meat stores, cook houses, dining rooms, ablutions, latrines, water storage tanks, pump houses, and wells. As most camps consisted of timber huts, generally the only indication of the location of a camp is a series of rectangular levelled earth platforms, or rows of brick or concrete pad stones to support the timber huts. Some camps, however, were built with permanent brick or concrete structures like Godwin Battery and Green Battery, both parts of the Spurn Head defences in East Yorkshire. The batteries on the islands in the Forth were like small villages, with numerous buildings to service the guns, searchlights, telephone system and the hospital.

Anti-submarine booms were first developed in August 1914 by Captain Munro, the officer in charge of the Invergordon naval base, working in conjunction with a local contractor in Inverness. While initially dismissed by the Admiralty, they were quickly adopted. Boom defence anchorages are very difficult to identify as they usually consist of nothing more than a substantial steel ring or bollard set in a large concrete block; such things are common near a port and may have served all manner of purposes, although one has been identified at Dale, Pembrokeshire. In shallow water anti-submarine nets would be slung from 'dolphins' – massive timbers set on the bed of the estuary. Occasionally, for instance at Scapa Flow, the remains of the nets, in the form of steel wire rings, survive drawn up on the shore.

Torpedo Batteries were installed at a number of locations, generally at the entrance to a harbour or where a channel narrows and an attacking ship would find it difficult to manoeuvre. It is very difficult to identify the site of a torpedo tube, as generally the only impression left is a holdfast ring of steel bolts.

Wireless stations and intelligence

Some of the first people in Britain to hear about the outbreak of the Great War were wireless operators who heard the British declaration of war upon Germany and her allies via Marconi long-distance wireless transmissions. The message declaring the outbreak of war was received by commercial and General Post Office staff as well as maritime wireless officers and wireless amateurs. In 1914, wireless telegraphy was less than twenty years old – it had been first developed commercially by Marconi and his eponymous wireless company in Britain in 1897 – and remained a system of point-to-point communication using Morse code. It was mostly used for maritime and long-distance communication but was still relatively experimental. Long-distance wireless stations such as those operated by the Marconi Company were licensed alongside smaller wireless stations, as well as experimental wireless stations belonging to amateurs. Furthermore, there were wireless stations operated by the General Post Office – who managed the state telecommunications monopoly – and the British military, in particular the Admiralty.

Figure 4.14 Marconi's historic wireless station at Poldhu, Cornwall, scene of the first transatlantic radio transmission in December 1901 (Courtesy of Elizabeth Bruton)

In 1914, the Marconi Company had long-distance wireless stations at Leafield, near Oxford, Chelmsford, Poldhu (Fig 4.14), Caernarfon, and Marconi House, London. Other, smaller, wireless companies such as the Lodge-Muirhead Wireless Syndicate also had long-distance wireless stations operating in Britain, while minor inland wireless stations were operated by the General Post Office.

At their most basic, these wireless stations generally consisted of transmitting and receiving aerials, usually made of metal but sometimes with wooden antennas, as well as a hut to house the wireless apparatus. Larger wireless stations might have a large concrete foundation as well as a more permanent, concrete wireless hut and other buildings including staff accommodation and a power station, since long-distance wireless stations required their own electricity generator. In addition to these permanent wireless stations, there were a number of temporary, experimental and sometimes mobile wireless stations which have left no physical trace.

At the outbreak of war, Britain had access to the 'All Red' cable telegraphy network, spanning both the Empire and the globe, and so had a cautious attitude to wireless telegraphy. Instead, long-distance wireless stations along the British coastline were used to send propaganda and news messages and to intercept and monitor domestic and enemy wireless traffic (Fig 4.15). In addition, wireless direction-finding stations were developed during the war to intercept wireless messages sent from enemy vessels, airships and boats, and hence calculate their positions. This combination of direction finding and signals interception came under the supervision of the Admiralty's Intelligence Division in 'Room 40' at the Admiralty which became the centre for signals intelligence and code breaking during the war and afterwards.

Figure 4.15 The transmitter / receiver building of the Admiralty wireless station at Pembroke Dock, still in use as a radar station by the Milford Haven Port Authority
(© R J C Thomas)

The effectiveness of Signals Intelligence (SIGINT) was made apparent in 1916 with notable successes including the interception of messages from German airships and bombers, and detecting that the German High Seas Fleet had left harbour prior to the Battle of Jutland in 1916. By 1917 a turning point had been reached, with more U-boats sunk and Zeppelins downed than in any previous year, mostly due to wireless interception and decryption. By 1918, 'Room 40' guaranteed Britain comprehensive access to the airwaves and during the first four months of the year four Zeppelins were shot down over England and 24 U-boats were sunk.

Few wireless stations from the early 20th century, including the First World War, have survived and the remains can be hard to discern. This is in part due to the nature of the wireless stations themselves: during this period many were temporary or experimental. In addition, the technology was relatively embryonic and developed rapidly – older wireless stations were easily dismantled, demolished, replaced, or reused. What has survived are wireless sets, key wireless aerials (for example, the post-war 2LO transmitter is held by the Science Museum), and a few sites. The concrete foundations of the Marconi station at Poldhu in Cornwall are still in place, as is the electricity generator building for the Marconi station at Hunstanton, Norfolk (Fig 4.16). Wireless huts at Lizard and nearby Mullion in Cornwall dating from before the First World War also remain in place.

Figure 4.16
Aerial view of the lighthouse and radio intercept station at Hunstanton, Norfolk. Established by amateur radio enthusiasts, the station was to provide vital intelligence to the military throughout the war (© English Heritage: Aerofilms Collection)

4.3 Naval dockyards and shipyards

At the outbreak of war Britain possessed the world's most powerful navy. It was a supremacy underpinned by the Edwardian heavy engineering industry in the country's naval dockyards and massive private yards that also competed to meet the demands of other aspiring nations. Most of Britain's naval dockyards dated back to the 17th century or earlier: Portsmouth, Chatham, Devonport, Sheerness and Pembroke were all sited to counter threats from the Continent and all of these yards were largely in their final form by 1906, barring extensions and alterations.

During the second half of Queen Victoria's reign and the early Edwardian era the three main royal dockyards at Chatham, Devonport and Portsmouth were greatly enlarged, adding considerable capacity. Portsmouth gained three large basins, five dry docks, and two locks which could also serve as dry docks. Chatham gained three new basins and four dry docks. Devonport saw the addition of two new basins, three dry docks and a lock which could also be used as a dry dock – this was the last of the great extensions and was completed in 1906 (Fig 4.17). Thereafter, with the advent of the Dreadnoughts and the growth in size of the navy, the facilities required some alterations and additions. At Portsmouth in 1906 only No 15 Dock could accommodate *Dreadnought* and this was the dock she entered during fitting out. Plans were made for two new locks and a new pumping station: C Lock opened in April 1913, D Lock in April 1914, and in addition No 14 Dock was lengthened in 1914. A 32,000-ton lift floating dock, originally installed at Portsmouth in 1912, was moved to Invergordon in September 1914. In 1906 Devonport was better served than Portsmouth, having three new docks which could accommodate Dreadnoughts. Chatham meanwhile specialised in the construction of submarines. Pembroke was the smallest of the royal dockyards and specialised in the construction and repair of light cruisers, submarines and other small vessels. During the First World War the workloads

Figure 4.17 A destroyer entering No 5 Dock at Devonport, probably in the early 1900s (Courtesy of Paul Brown)

Figure 4.18 HM Monitor *M33* seen in No 1 Dock at Portsmouth. HMS *M33* is one of only a handful of surviving ships from the First World War and forms part of the Historic National Fleet (© Paul Brown)

in the yards increased greatly, and the total dockyard workforce grew from 45,600 to 93,370.

In all three of the main yards many of the buildings and most of the basins, dry docks and locks remain and are largely unaltered from their First World War appearance. At both Portsmouth and Devonport many of these facilities are still in use and public access is very limited. Access to part of the historic, largely Georgian, dockyard at Portsmouth is possible at all times, but the Edwardian and Victorian areas are still in use and can only be accessed on rare Open Days (Fig 4.18). At Devonport, Keyham Yard (now owned by Babcock) is generally inaccessible except for occasional guided tours but South Yard is more accessible as it is now little-used by the navy. At Chatham the historic, largely Georgian, part of the dockyard is open to visitors at all times and the Victorian extension has been redeveloped for commercial shipping, yacht marinas, and urban development: the most interesting part, by Basin No 1, is readily accessible. Pembroke dockyard closed during the 1920s and is now largely covered by industrial development, although a few dockyard buildings remain.

In Scotland, the use of two (later three) large floating docks at the Invergordon naval base allowed maintenance on the largest battleships. In Ireland, the

Buncrana Naval Base on Lough Swilly provided a good anchorage on the north coast of Ireland, giving adequate protection for the Royal Naval Fleet during 1914–18. In fact the British Grand Fleet spent some time in Lough Swilly during October 1914, availing itself of the Lough's substantial defences and the safety of the port, along with its well-organised and controlled approaches.

The Harland and Wolff Yard in Belfast meanwhile provided maintenance for the Royal Navy, with the docking capacity to take in vessels to the size of Dreadnoughts for maintenance and repairs.

Rosyth: a new dockyard

Early in the 20th century, a burgeoning German navy posed a potential threat from across the North Sea. Thus a new naval base and dockyard on the east coast was deemed necessary, capable of handling the largest warships. For this, a 1470 acre (c 600ha) site on the north shore of the Firth of Forth, just west of the Forth Rail Bridge, was selected in 1903 although the main construction contract was not let until February 1909, for completion in seven years. It was to be built in stages, with the Admiralty progressively taking over completed works. The new dockyard comprised a large, non-tidal basin of 56 acres (c 22ha) accessed via an entrance lock, with three dry docks leading off the north side of the basin (each 850 x 110ft (259 x 33m)), a tidal basin suitable for small craft like submarines and destroyers, plus supporting workshops and facilities. Unlike Portsmouth, Devonport and Chatham, no 'new build' facilities were included.

The main contractor was Easton, Gibb & Son Ltd, who undertook what was

Figure 4.19 Plan of Rosyth Dockyard from the Admiralty Dock Book 1914 (Courtesy of Ian Buxton)

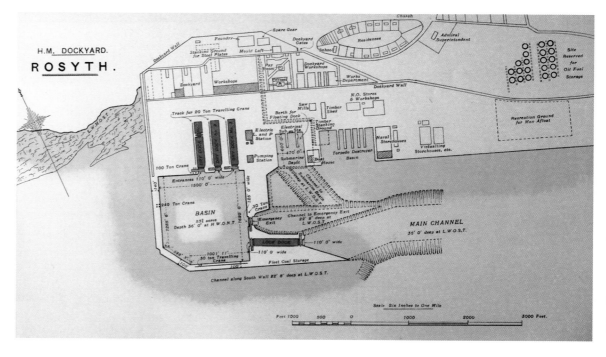

H.M. DOCKYARD, ROSYTH.
TESTING 250 TONS CRANE.
VIEW FROM WEST WALL OF MAIN BASIN, LOOKING NORTH.   5·7·17   T 70

Figure 4.20 The 250 ton cantilever crane at Rosyth (© RCAHMS: Sir William Arrol Collection)

probably the largest civil engineering contract at the time in the UK. The dockyard extended past the existing shoreline into deeper water, requiring embankments to allow work to proceed in the dry. Substantial concrete monoliths were sunk to create the walls of the basin. The dry docks were excavated, partly through rock, to a depth allowing battleships drawing 38ft (11.5m) to enter. Approach channels were dredged to 45ft (13.7m), deep enough to allow a damaged battleship to enter. The basin and dry dock walls and copings were all lined with Norwegian granite (Fig 4.19).

Although the submarine basin was largely complete on the outbreak of the First World War, much had yet to be done on the main basin, dry docks, and associated facilities. Despite shortages of labour, the basin was flooded in September 1915, but the entrance lock and the first dry dock (No 1, the westernmost) were not completed until six months later. The first warship to use them was the battleship *Zealandia*, which entered No 1 Dock on 27 March 1916. No 2 Dock was finished in April, which allowed capital ships damaged at the Battle of Jutland to be repaired at Rosyth from June. Most of the remaining facilities were completed in 1916–17, including workshops, slipways for small craft, a railway system linking to the main line at Inverkeithing, and a 250 ton cantilever crane (Fig 4.20). The latter, completed in 1917, was located on the west wall and was capable of lifting heavy gun and machinery components. A similar 100 ton crane was completed in 1920 on the north wall. The three main groups of workshops were sited north of the dry docks: eight bays for the construction department, two bays for the boilermakers and seven bays for the engineering department. These steel-framed, brick-faced shops still stand but were later used for steelwork fabrication, railway stock overhaul, and weapons and electronics maintenance respectively. The new naval base and dockyard provided valuable facilities for the Royal Navy's Grand Fleet, based at Scapa Flow, only one day's steaming from Rosyth. During the First World War, no fewer than 83 battleships passed through its dry docks.

With the post-war rundown of the Royal Navy, there was less need for the new dockyard, so it was put on care and maintenance in 1925. Parts were leased out for shipbreaking, with Metal Industries breaking up ships ranging from trawlers to transatlantic liners (eg *Mauretania*, *Leviathan*). Ten German battleships salvaged at Scapa Flow after their scuttling in 1919 were broken up between 1928 and 1939, all but one in one of the dry docks. The dockyard was brought back into full Admiralty use in 1939, its facilities much as they were in 1918.

What remains of the original Rosyth dockyard today? The main basin, Nos 2 and 3 Docks and the entrance lock look much as they did, albeit with upgraded facilities. No 1 Dock has been extensively rebuilt and has been used to assemble the Royal Navy's two new aircraft carriers. The three main groups of workshops still stand, but are now used for different purposes. Much of the stone-walled structure of the electrical generating station and dry dock pumphouse still stand immediately to the east of No 3 Dock. What have gone are all the original cranes, the small craft facilities east of the main basin, oil storage tanks further east, and most of the smaller buildings.

Naval armament depots

At the beginning of the war Britain's main naval armament depots were at Plymouth, Portsmouth, Marchwood (Southampton) and Chatham; locations facing the country's traditional foes of France and Holland (Fig 4.21). After August 1914 the focus of naval forces shifted eastwards and northwards to the North Sea and the fleet anchorages at Invergordon and Scapa Flow, Orkney. At Portsmouth, just prior to the outbreak of war a new store depot opened at Bedenham, while the old establishment at Priddy's Hard was left to concentrate on cartridge and shell filling, including with the new high-explosive amatol. To serve the new dockyard at Rosyth and the Scapa Flow base a depot was built at Crombie on the Forth as well as a smaller store upriver at Bandeath. Smaller facilities were also established at Buncrana, Milford Haven, Harwich, Dover and Liverpool; at the last three some of the stores were kept afloat while temporary depots were established elsewhere. Mine depots were built at Bedenham (Hants), at Inverness and Invergordon (for the US Navy), and at Grangemouth. Prior to the war most naval armaments had been moved by ship, but the threat of attack by U-boats forced more traffic onto the railways and branch lines were extended

into the depots. Provision was also needed to assemble and store novel devices including depth charges, explosive paravanes used in anti-submarine operations, mine clearance paravanes, and aerial bombs. At Priddy's Hard the arrival of women was reflected in the construction of separate changing and dining rooms, latrines, and a matron's block.

Shipbuilding

In addition to the large naval dockyards there were important private shipbuilding yards at Belfast, Barrow, and on the rivers Mersey, Tyne, and Clyde. In Belfast, Harland & Wolff shipyard reassigned its work from traditional ship and liner construction to ship conversions along with the building and repair of new warships for the Royal Navy. These included the battlecruiser *Glorious*; the *Vindictive* (modified to carry aircraft); and the 48,000-ton hospital ship *Britannic* which was later sunk in the Aegean Sea. Furthermore, during this 'boom-time' Harland & Wolff required a second yard, resulting in the construction of the Musgrave Yard. Many minor shipyards were also kept busy maintaining and repairing smaller coastal vessels, including inland yards serving canal traffic. One novel development of the war was the construction of concrete barges, a move that saved timber and steel; a number of these survive as stranded hulks.

Scapa Flow, Orkney

From late July 1914, when the Grand Fleet sailed north in secrecy to its designated war station, Scapa Flow became the principal wartime anchorage for Britain's surface fleet until April 1918, when Admiral Beatty made Rosyth and the Forth estuary the Grand Fleet's main base. Popularly dubbed 'the stopper in the North Sea bottle', Scapa Flow combined the advantages of a strategic controlling location with those of an expansive anchorage with much sea room for manoeuvres.

Virtually defenceless in August 1914, by mid-1915 the anchorage was equipped with a relatively secure shore-based and underwater defence network comprising coast batteries, anti-submarine and anti-destroyer boom nets, blockships, indicator loops, hydrophones and controlled minefields. Organised into two fire commands, the shore-based defences were centred around thirteen coast batteries, of which there are surviving visible remains of all but two, some still very well defined (Fig 4.22). Between September 1914 and October 1915, 23 vessels, amounting to over 50,000 gross tons of shipping, were sunk as blockships across five vulnerable access channels. Of these First World War blockships, the most recognisable survivor is the stern section of the *Reginald*, an 1878 coastal passenger cargo vessel which lies in East Weddel Sound. Distorted remnants of a mile-long fixed barrier built of bolted steel rails across the main approach from the north-west also still remain at the bottom of Clestrain Sound.

A few vestiges survive of the airship station, kite balloon station and five seaplane bases that were established here for submarine reconnaissance purposes. The field that served as a naval aviation practice strip at Smoogro is also identifiable;

Figure 4.22 Coast Battery, Roan Head, Flotta: aerial view from east showing typical layout of gun emplacements and access trenches to semi-subterranean magazine, three early 1915 'puny' 3-pounder guns having been replaced here in 1916 by four 12-pounders, June 1997
(© RCAHMS)

Figure 4.23 Anti-Aircraft Battery, Burray Ness, Burray: view of one of the two gun holdfasts and magazine from east, July 1998
(© Geoffrey Stell)

Figure 4.24 Former paravane and torpedo depot, Lyness, Hoy, converted to a NAAFI and cinema in the Second World War, and now the largest surviving First World War structure in Orkney: view from north-east, June 2014 (© Michael Taylor)

it was from here, in August 1917, that Commander Dunning flew to make an historic, first-ever deck landing onto a moving ship. Structural remains of the first two anti-aircraft batteries to be established in Orkney in 1917–18 also still survive, that on Burray Ness being the most complete of this period in Scotland (Fig 4.23).

First located at Scapa itself, the administrative headquarters of the Admiral Commanding Orkney and Shetland moved to the still-extant Longhope Hotel on South Walls in late 1914. For most of the war, however, logistical support for the fleet – coaling, oiling, arming, repairing, refitting, administering, accommodating – was carried out afloat, not ashore, and it was not until September 1916 that Treasury approval was granted for a major stores, fuel and ordnance depot at Lyness on Hoy. Beginning with the construction of a wharf that was estimated to take fifteen months, the programme also included four 8000-ton oil storage tanks, petrol tanks, a power house, paravane and torpedo depots, storage sheds, workers' camps, and two reservoirs. Repair facilities for smaller vessels were also introduced in early 1917 in the form of a floating dock for destroyers.

Much of the construction work at Lyness continued after the Armistice, but by late 1920 the anchorage had been closed and the naval headquarters transferred to Invergordon. One of the four original oil tanks and the big sheds that began life as paravane and torpedo depots have survived the later development and subsequent closure (in 1957) of the Lyness base (Fig 4.24).

From November 1918 Scapa Flow became the anchorage for the internment of 74 surface vessels of the German High Seas Fleet which, on the well-concealed orders of Admiral von Reuter, were dramatically scuttled on 21 June 1919 (Fig 4.25). Sunk beyond economic salvage in the deepest water, seven major German ships, four cruisers and three battleships still survive as wrecks; digital three-dimensional virtual models of them can be viewed on the Scapa Flow Marine Archaeology Project website at http://www.scapamap.org/.

Figure 4.25 A postcard showing the scuttling of German Destroyers at Scapa Flow (Courtesy of Wayne Cocroft)

4.4 Ships and submarine wrecks

Archaeological overview

Studies of the First World War rarely include acknowledgement of archaeological remains found offshore, yet victory in continental Europe would never have been achieved had the war at sea not been efficaciously prosecuted by Britain and her allies. Sites, monuments and seascapes directly linked to the daily struggle for maritime supremacy and safe passage survive in contexts accessible to those few who are able to visit them (Fig 4.26).

A very high percentage of known and dated shipwreck losses around the UK's inshore waters occurred during the First World War. As will be shown, the extensive remains of fishing boats, merchant and naval shipwreck sites, sunken submarines, minefields, navigational infrastructure and early naval aviation sites provide evidence of this under-investigated resource (Fig 4.27).

Figure 4.26 The guns of HMS *Audacious*, which was sunk 27 October 1914 by a German mine in Lough Swilly, off the north coast of Ireland (© Leigh Bishop)

Figure 4.27 Sonar image of the SMS *Markgraf*, the most impressive of the König class battleships in Scapa Flow. The wreck remains in superb condition (Courtesy of ScapaMap)

Historical context

It had been expected that the outbreak of war on 4 August 1914 would lead to a shattering Trafalgar-like battle between the British Grand Fleet and the German High Seas Fleet with the Royal Navy emerging triumphant. As the war progressed, naval strategy became characterised by the tenacious efforts of the Allied Powers, with their larger fleets and surrounding position, to blockade the Central Powers, and the efforts of the Central Powers to break that blockade and to establish an effective blockade of the UK and France through the use of submarines and raiders.

A key component of British naval strategy of the First World War was to deny passage of the German High Seas Fleet to the Atlantic through the English Channel and the North Sea. The Admiralty realised that the German High Command would inevitably try to slip their battleships based at Kiel and Wilhelmshaven out to the Atlantic by the northern route through the North Sea. The perfect base to maintain guard over this passage was at Scapa Flow in Orkney and while the Admiralty had taken an interest in that anchorage as early as 1905, the base was not rendered fully secure against attack until November 1914, following penetration of the German submarine U-18.

However, the German surface fleet was far from being confined to port, for German warships bombarded Scarborough, Whitby and Hartlepool in December 1914 and at each location escaped retaliation from the Royal Navy (see Fig 3.1). Major engagements were to follow at Dogger Bank (January 1915 and February 1916), Jutland (May/June 1916) and Heligoland Bight (November 1917).

In February 1915, Germany declared the waters around the British Isles to be a war zone, with merchant ships – Allied and neutral alike – subject to attack. Against this background, the war at sea had, for mariners in home waters, become focused on the principal theatres of the North Sea, the English Channel and the Atlantic Ocean. The following sections address the five broad types of service (Royal Naval Air Service, Royal Naval Reserve, Mercantile Marine, Royal Navy surface fleet and the submarine service) and seek to recall summary histories through assessment of the surviving evidence.

Royal Naval Air Service

The Admiralty had developed its own air service from 1912, with the Royal Naval Air Service's seaplane base on the Isle of Grain and airship station at Kingsnorth established by August 1914. Before war began, aircraft had participated in manoeuvres with the Royal Navy using the converted cruiser *Hermes* as a seaplane carrier. (*Hermes* was later sunk by *U-27* on 31 October 1914 with the loss of 22 of her crew, some 22 miles east of Dover where her remains have been identified at a depth of 30m.)

By the outbreak of war, the RNAS had 93 aircraft, six airships and two balloons but the use of air power at sea was largely confined to patrol and reconnaissance roles rather than in direct combat. In the air, convoys were protected by aircraft such as the Felixstowe F2A Flying Boat which operated out of bases like those at Felixstowe and Yarmouth. The F2As frequently engaged German seaplanes in an attempt to maintain control of the air in the southern North Sea. The RNAS also conducted the official trials of the then largest aircraft to have been built in the UK: the Handley Page O/100 bomber, which from September 1917 was used on anti-submarine patrols off the River Tees.

The remains of naval air stations survive at places like Tresco (Isles of Scilly), Killingholme, Seaton Carew and South Shields. In addition, naval airships provided aerial observation of German submarines threatening shipping and convoys in the North Sea and the English Channel. A section of one of the airship sheds survives at Moat Farm in St Mary Hoo, Medway.

Of the aircraft themselves, no RNAS airframes are known to survive archaeologically as they were light, relatively flimsy and, with airframes of wood and 'doped' (varnished) fabric, particularly susceptible to fire. However, crash-sites are recorded such as the loss of a seaplane off Lyme Bay, Dorset in November 1916.

At sea, the RNAS made use of vessels like Seaplane Lighter *H21* (built 1918) to support seaborne aircraft operations. *H21* now forms part of the National Historic Fleet (administered by National Historic Ships UK) and is stored at the Fleet Air Arm Museum, Yeovilton.

Minesweepers and Royal Naval Reserve

Before the outbreak of war, sea mines had been identified as being a threat to Britain's shipping, and efforts were begun to counter the threat. Fishing trawlers were recognised as having an affinity with mine clearance, owing to their trawl gear, and a trawler section of the Royal Naval Reserve was soon established (Fig 4.28; see also Fig 6.2). The first vessels of the section were the Flower-class minesweeping sloops, of which 72 were built under the emergency war programme. Surprisingly few were lost during the war but one casualty was HMS *Lavender* which lies in the English Channel having been sunk by *UC-75* in May 1917.

Recent analysis of minesweeping off England's east coast has revealed evidence associated with the East Coast War Channels – a suite of carefully defined routes that were swept of mines between the Thames and the border with Scotland in both the First and Second World Wars. These routes formed the main seaways for the vast amount of civilian shipping that was necessary to meet the country's domestic needs and to continue fighting. The channels were swept by minesweepers and an array of other minor warships was engaged in maintaining and defending traffic. An extensive range of archaeological evidence survives related to the War Channels' infrastructure: sweeping, routing, escorts, defensive mining, coastal forces, lights and buoys, salvage and clearance; all require further research and assessment.

In addition, some sloops were designed as submarine decoys – the Q-ships – which had a distinctive merchant marine appearance but with hidden armament. Developed from disguising armed trawlers as early as

Figure 4.28 Cigarette manufacturers produced numerous series of cards depicting the Forces; this one shows the Royal Naval Reserve (Courtesy of Mark Dunkley)

WILLS'S CIGARETTES.

A TRIBUTE TO THE MINE SWEEPERS AND R.N.R. WORK.

1915, the Q-ships operated from Queenstown in Ireland and Granton on the Forth. Some 366 Q-ships are thought to have been in operation during the war, of which 61 were sunk. The only surviving Q-ship is the Flower-class sloop HMS *President* (formerly HMS *Saxifrage*; built 1917) moored on the Victoria Embankment in London. The *President* forms part of the UK's National Historic Fleet.

Mercantile Marine

During the First World War, as with the Second, ships of the mercantile marine lay within a wider system concerned not only with ensuring that there were sufficient ships to provide the transport necessary for the effective prosecution of the war, but also enough ships to protect them. Civilian shipping, inclusive of those engaged in coastal trades (ie fishermen, lightship operators and pilots), was attacked throughout both wars.

By September 1915, U-boats had sunk 480 merchant vessels in home waters including the Cunard liner *Lusitania*, which was torpedoed off the Irish coast in May 1915 with the loss of *c* 1200 men, women and children. Losses of merchant ships were to become critical, with the majority falling on those engaged in ocean-going trade. Unrestricted submarine warfare was announced by Germany on 9 January 1917. A belated defensive response to this was the introduction of a convoy system from April of that year and the construction of a growing number of dedicated escort vessels to supplement fleet destroyers.

Another class of civilian shipping taken up from the trade were the hospital ships. Largely converted from oceanic liners built in the early years of the 20th century, hospital ships formed part of the essential system that linked wounded personnel on the Western Front with military hospitals in Britain. (Siegfried Sassoon, for example, records his passage on the hospital ship *Aberdonian* from Rouen to Southampton in August 1916, following action during the Battle of the Somme.) Despite their red crosses, hospital ships were not immune to attack: the SS *Anglia*, for example, was mined off Folkestone in November 1915 with the loss of 134 people, including wounded officers and soldiers, while the SS *Glenart Castle* was torpedoed by *UC-56* in the Bristol Channel in February 1918 with the loss of 162 people including medical staff.

Reports received by the Board of Trade relating to casualties of non-naval British-registered trading vessels, yachts and fishing vessels as well as the deaths of seamen and passengers during the war were published in 1921. These revealed that during the period 1 July 1914 to 31 December 1918 the number of vessels totally lost by marine casualty (eg collision, missing, strandings and founderings) numbered 915, compared to 3781 vessels lost by enemy action. Of the total losses to British-registered merchant and fishing vessels during the four and a half years of the war, 80.5% were losses due to enemy action. The number of crew and passengers killed on merchant and fishing vessels during the war is recorded as 21,886. In addition to four seamen reported to have been killed by bombs from enemy aircraft, one was executed, 67 died while interned as PoWs in enemy countries and two released PoWs died in Holland after removal from Germany.

Naval surface units

The naval armaments race leading up to the First World War led to both Britain and Germany (as well as the US, France, Italy and Japan) building warships of previously unknown size and power. Britain's naval dockyards and commercial shipbuilding industry were out-producing those of Germany with big-gun capital ships, cruisers, smaller warships, support vessels, depot ships and lesser craft numbering more than any other power, and the Royal Navy was also able to draw reserve strength from the world's largest merchant navy and fishing fleet.

For the British, the armament race culminated in the *Dreadnought*, launched in February 1906, which was the first large warship to be turbine driven. Very heavily armed and high-powered, she rendered all earlier battleships obsolete. Innovation continued, and in 1912 HMS *Bristol* became the first warship to run on superheated steam from her twelve boilers, enabling even greater speeds as well as fuel economies.

While there was some general progress in marine engineering during the years of the First World War, the Admiralty pursued a policy of caution and concentrated on simplifying machinery layout. As the war progressed, the main problem was to keep ships at sea or in a state of constant readiness. Maintenance had to be reduced to a minimum and rapid repair through the use of small-scale welding was introduced from 1917 as an alternative to the standard practice of riveting hull plates together

General modifications made to warships during the war included a change from coal to oil fuel for most new warships, heightened fore-funnels to keep bridgework clear of smoke and gases, the addition of balloons and aircraft, and the installation of anti-aircraft guns. Depth charges and anti-submarine howitzers (such as that from the former armoured cruiser HMS *Leviathan* in the reserve collection at the Museum of Naval Firepower, Gosport) were also later additions. Various means of obscuring ship features in order to confuse the silhouette were employed from April 1915, such as a painted false bow wave and, later, dazzle camouflage painting, to make coincidence range-finding more difficult (see Fig 4.18).

The light cruiser *Amphion* was the first Royal Navy ship to be sunk in the war; she was mined in the outer Thames Estuary on 6 August 1914. Some 150 sailors and eighteen German prisoners were killed. The wreck is a protected military maritime grave.

An understanding of the lines, layout and structure of a First World War warship can be seen in HMS *Caroline*, the last remaining light cruiser. *Caroline* saw action at the Battle of Jutland in 1916 before being paid-off in 1922 and later becoming a naval reserve headquarters ship in Belfast Harbour, where she remains. The only other confirmed naval survivors of the war are the monitor HMS *M33* at Portsmouth, the sloop *President* (ex *Saxifrage*) on the Thames and the torpedo boat CMB4 at Duxford. All four survivors form part of the UK's National Historic Fleet.

Submarine losses

The gasoline-powered *U-15*, a Type U 13 U-boat, was the first submarine casualty of the war: it was rammed and sunk by the British light cruiser HMS *Birmingham* on 9 August 1914 in the North Sea with the loss of all hands. The engines of *U-15* had apparently failed as she was lying stopped on the surface in heavy fog when *Birmingham* spotted her; hammering could clearly be heard from inside the boat, presumably from attempted repairs. The cruiser fired on her but missed, and as *U-15* began to dive, *Birmingham* rammed her, cutting her in two. A further 204 U-boats were either rammed, mined, torpedoed or sunk by gunfire during the war.

Recent research commissioned by Historic England records the fact that 44 U-boats were lost in England's inshore region (that is, areas of the ocean generally within 12 nautical miles of the coast) (Fig 4.29). Just over one fifth of all U-boat losses from the war therefore lie within 12 nm of England's coastline, comprising types that were launched throughout the whole war. Only two of these U-boats are protected as military maritime graves – *UB-65* and *UB-81*. Access to these two submarines is restricted by the Ministry of Defence.

Perhaps unsurprisingly, British submarine losses largely lie further afield, having been lost in operations overseas. Only three are known to have sunk during the war close to the English coast – *C29* (accidentally mined in the Humber estuary, August 1915), *D5* (mined off Great Yarmouth, November 1914) and *E6* (mined off Harwich, December 1915) – while in Scotland the so-called 'Battle of the Island of May' at the mouth of the Firth of Forth early in 1918 saw a series of collisions between Royal Navy surface ships and submarines, during which two K Class submarines were lost, with the death of 104 men, and three others were damaged.

Figure 4.29 The remains of a U-boat lying in the mud of the Medway Estuary, Kent in 2011 (© English Heritage)

Protection of the Underwater Cultural Heritage

Since 4 August 2014, submerged archaeological remains associated with the First World War now fall under the aegis of the 2001 UNESCO Convention on the Protection of the Underwater Cultural Heritage. Such remains have not yet been comprehensively researched despite the fact that they relate directly to one of the most important conflicts in recent history. Their archaeological importance is not well defined and they remain vulnerable to metal recovery, souvenir- and treasure-hunting and the poorly understood long-term effects of oceanic climate change.

One hundred years following the commencement of the First World War, extensive remains from the conflict survive, largely intact, in, on or under the seabed. Responsible diver access to submerged remains of the First World War is encouraged as a means to identify, understand and record the largely forgotten stories of the struggle in the seas surrounding the UK. Diving, however, must follow established codes of conduct, such as UNESCO's *Code of Ethics for Diving on Underwater Cultural Heritage Sites* and be undertaken only after thorough training. For those wishing to become involved more deeply, guidance is available from a number of organisations involved in promoting nautical archaeology.

Military maritime graves

The Protection of Military Remains Act 1986 (PMRA), administered by the Ministry of Defence, applies both to the remains of service personnel and also to the vessels and aircraft in which they were lost. It secures them from unauthorized interference and is thus an important means of protection. Remains fall under two headings: protected places and controlled sites. Wrecks are designated by name and can be designated as protected places even if the location of the site is not known. Thus, the wreckage of a UK military aircraft is automatically a protected place even if the physical remains have not been previously discovered or identified. Shipwrecks need to be specifically designated, and designation as a protected place applies only to vessels that sank after 4 August 1914. The Act makes it an offence to interfere with a protected place, to disturb the site or to remove anything from it.

Divers may visit the site but the rule is look, don't touch and don't penetrate. Controlled sites containing the remains of an aircraft or a vessel that crashed, sank or was stranded within the last two hundred years must be specifically designated by location. The Act makes it illegal to conduct any operations (including any diving or excavation) within the controlled site that might disturb the remains unless licensed to do so by the Ministry of Defence. Controlled sites at sea are marked on Admiralty charts and their physical location is marked by means of a buoy.

CHAPTER 5

Air

5.1 Introduction

Military flying in its formative stages was fostered by a high degree of government and commercial collaboration, along with popular and press enthusiasm: aviation had a strong voice through the Aero Club, the Aeronautical Society and specialist journals such as *Flight* (1909) and *The Aeroplane* (1911). The civilian flying schools at Larkhill in Wiltshire and Eastchurch in Kent, both of which retain hangars dating from 1910, played a key role in the training of army and navy pilots. In April 1911 the War Office's Air Battalion was formed, absorbing the Royal Engineers' Balloon School, and established at the Royal Aircraft Factory in Farnborough. The foundation in April 1912 of the Royal Flying Corps (RFC) prompted the establishment of three key sites: under development from 1912 was Upavon for officer training and Netheravon as the RFC's prototype squadron base, both sited close to the army's training areas on Salisbury Plain, and also Montrose, on the east coast of Scotland. The Admiralty had already begun work on a chain of coastal stations prior to the foundation early in 1914 of the Royal Naval Air Service (RNAS) (see Chapter 4) for working with the Fleet in home waters.

The RFC and RNAS continued on separate paths for much of the First World War, during which time there was increasing recognition of the potential of air power as an independent part of the armed forces. The Smuts Report, compiled in the aftermath of the Gotha bomber raids on coastal towns in Kent and then London in the summer of 1917, paved the way for the unification of both services into the Royal Air Force in April 1918 and the establishment of a unified command structure, with intercept squadrons and anti-aircraft guns placed outside London. The RAF's first Chief of Air Staff, General Sir Hugh Trenchard, concentrated upon developing its strategic role as an offensive bomber force.

By November 1918 the RAF occupied 301 sites. In addition to 60 airship stations and 14 balloon operations stations (see below), these included:

- 45 RAF Schools, including 23 aerodromes and 4 balloon stations, for technical training ranging from engineering (Halton) to armaments (Uxbridge) and photography (Farnborough);
- 63 Training Depot Stations which were initiated in 1917 and absorbed earlier stations for training increasing numbers of pilots. The TDS scheme comprised the largest airfield construction programme of the period;

- 34 Home Defence Stations for the protection of London and the east coast as far north as Edinburgh and Fife, 29 Marine Operations Stations, 5 Landing Grounds and 2 Independent Force Stations for Trenchard's new strategic bomber force;
- 27 Aircraft Acceptance Parks, often served by their own railway lines, established in 1917 for the reception of aircraft from factories, and their storage, flight testing and distribution to operational squadrons;
- 11 Aircraft Repair Depots established in 1917 for training in the rapid repair of aircraft and aero engines and 5 Training and Repair Marine Operations Stations;
- 7 Experimental Stations;
- 19 Store Depots and Distribution Parks and 6 Mobilisation Stations.

5.2 Airfields and seaplane stations

From the earliest date the planning of air stations distinguished between the separate functional areas of domestic and technical sites, the latter with hangars which faced onto a grass flying field. Until the formation of the RAF, and the Air Ministry's Directorate of Works and Buildings, in April 1918 responsibility for design and construction was split between the War Office's Directorate of Fortifications and Works and the Admiralty's Directorate of Works. Both sought a degree of standardisation in design, through issuing standard specifications for building types against which contractors submitted tenders.

By 1918, standardised type designs catered for every aspect of airfield operation and life. The planning of technical buildings reflected the aircraft technology of the period, from bomb storage, synthetic training, motor transport and storage to carpenters', dope and engine-repair shops. Training Depot Stations, for example, had their technical sites split into four different sections, for aircraft, ground instruction, motor vehicles, and services. Their organising principle for domestic buildings has much in common with post-1850s barracks planning, particularly in its careful attention to hierarchies of rank through the provision of separate accommodation for officers and men. They also catered for a range of facilities from relaxation and socialising (institutes and sometimes cinemas) to shopping, laundry and providing a haircut. A distinctive new feature was the provision of separate accommodation for women.

Hangars

Hangars for housing aircraft are the most readily recognisable structures. The first generation of hangars had their doors opening from the side wall towards the flying field (Fig 5.1). The larger-span end-opening shed followed the decision taken in March 1916 to increase the number of aircraft in a squadron from twelve to eighteen (see Figs 5.2–4). These were typically paired together, only the repair

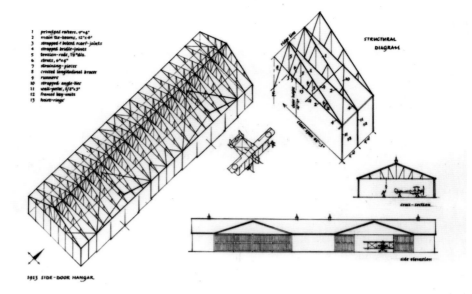

section hangar remaining as a single-span shed. Most RFC and RAF hangars were constructed from timber, lattice girders (so-called Belfast trusses; see Figs 3.4 & 5.3) being the most common form of construction. In contrast, the Admiralty continued to construct its side-opening hangars on seaplane stations out of steel (see p 126).

The most variation was in the choice of materials applied to these standard plans, evident for example in the planning of the airmen's and officers' accommodation built in 1913–14 at Upavon (concrete block) and Netheravon (asbestos panel with timber frame and cover strips). The most commonly encountered materials are brick laid to a single thickness (4.5 inches wide) with brick piers, and concrete block with timber or concrete wall posts, with roofs of corrugated asbestos or felt. The prefabricated, curved, corrugated-iron Nissen hut, designed in 1916 by Lt Col Peter Nissen, appears to have been used exclusively abroad and no First World War examples are known from Britain. Some sites, usually those of a specialist nature, were provided with bespoke materials or designs.

Survival

Many factors, in addition to the intended short life expectancy of most wartime buildings, have affected the survival of pre- and First World War aviation buildings. From the pre-war period, the headquarters building and balloon store of the Royal Engineers' Air Battalion, built after April 1911, has survived at Farnborough. Remarkably, hangars have survived from the pre-1912 flying schools at Larkhill and Eastchurch, as have extensive ranges of buildings dated 1913–14 from the Royal Flying Corps sites at Upavon and Netheravon, which are still in military use. Together with the early hangar suite of 1913 at Montrose in Scotland, these comprise survivals of great importance within a European and wider international context. The majority of sites (271) built during the war were disposed of afterwards, some such as Bicester and Scampton being later reoccupied by the RAF. There is only a handful of other sites which have retained their hangars, and later reuse was a critical factor in the survival of most buildings, as for example at RAF Leuchars. At the Loch Doon Aerial Gunnery School, the concrete foundations of both seaplane and airplane hangars survive, although the gunnery school was totally abandoned, partly due to poor drainage.

The RAF Museum at Hendon holds some airfield plans and drawings for RFC buildings, and plans of nearly all the sites documented in November 1918 can be found in The National Archives. Such sources need to be used with some care, as site plans can show the intended rather than the completed layout of buildings and site design. The website of the Airfield Research Group also contains a lot of useful information on First World War airfields and other sites. Sites with longer operational histories may also have experienced successive phases of rebuilding. One paired hangar has survived at Tadcaster, near York, from the Training Depot Station formed in July 1918 from an earlier fighter airfield (Fig 5.2), and similarly the recently demolished hangars at Hainault Farm in Essex dated from a rebuilding later in the war. Some hangars, as at Shrewsbury and Eastleigh, have been reclad and reused as industrial units and it was also common for hangars – especially the steel-built ones on seaplane stations – to be re-erected on other RAF bases and civilian sites, such as one next to the railway line at Wimbledon. At Drem airfield in East Lothian, three technical buildings as well as the officers' mess survive. Individual technical and domestic buildings might be hard to identify with confidence if the site has been substantially redeveloped, while those on rural sites can be found, for example,

Figure 5.2 First World War aircraft hangar at Tadcaster, Yorks. The building has been well maintained and remains in everyday use as a barn (© Catrina Appleby)

Figure 5.3 Diagram
of a Belfast truss
from Edgar Lucas'
Light Buildings (1935)
(Courtesy of
R J C Thomas)

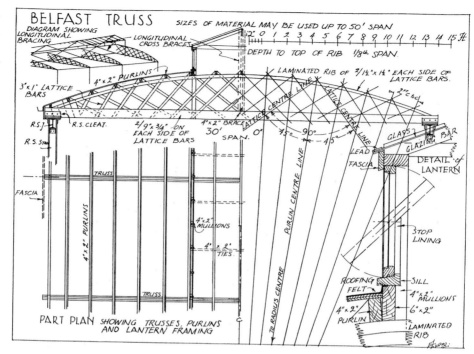

within later woodland. It was also common for roof trusses and, more rarely, substantial sections of buildings to be re-erected as covered cattle yards and other farm buildings. The wing of a First World War Handley Page O/400 bomber was found incorporated into the roof of a building at Dock Road, Connah's Quay. RNAS personnel, in particular officers, were frequently accommodated within houses and other buildings requisitioned for the duration of the war.

Catterick in North Yorkshire is the only example of a Home Defence Station to have retained its original suite of hangars, externally rebuilt around their steel-framed construction. Other significant survivals include Stow Maries in Essex, from which aircraft defended London against Zeppelins and Gotha bombers (see below), and the three 1917 General Service sheds at RFC North Shotwick, Flintshire. Another critical issue to consider in the assessment of sites is their historical associations and importance at a local as well as national level. Leighterton in Gloucestershire is one example of a site whose buildings have been removed and its flying field restored to farmland, but its small cemetery for pilots who perished in training has made it a focus of local events and commemoration for relatives and representatives of the Australians and New Zealanders who served there.

Recent work has shown that significant remains of First World War airfields do survive and in order to understand the likely remains, it is worth visiting examples of upstanding sites. Access to Upavon, Netheravon and some other key sites dating from the First World War is unfortunately restricted as they are in military use. Eastchurch is in use as a prison, and many other sites are in commercial use. Some can be clearly viewed from publicly accessible roads, such

Figure 5.4 General
Service Shed at Old
Sarum (© Wayne
Cocroft)

as the three seaplane sheds built in 1918 for a Training Depot Station and which are grouped around the original slipway at Lee-on-Solent. Careful comparison of the November 1918 maps of most RAF stations with modern maps can reveal unexpected survivals: at Donibristle in Fife a group of a dozen or so First World War buildings has recently been identified 'hiding' in a corner of a light industrial estate on a former aerodrome. Meanwhile at nearby RAF Leuchars, it has become clear that many more buildings than originally thought were constructed in 1914–18. Examination of woodland or rough ground around aerodromes may reveal the remains of structures that have escaped later damage.

Set out below are some of the most significant and representative sites which are wholly or partly accessible to the public, largely due to the efforts of local groups and enthusiasts.

The Imperial War Museum site at Duxford near Cambridge was mostly rebuilt in the 1930s but retains the best-preserved group of technical buildings representative of a Training Depot Station dating from October 1917, including three paired hangars which played a starring role in the *Battle of Britain* film – when the repair hangar was blown up!

A café with a terrace overlooks the airfield at Old Sarum near Salisbury. Two paired hangars and a repair hangar of 1917 design, along with other technical buildings, relate to the least-altered flying field of the period up to November 1918 (Fig 5.4).

Farnborough in Hampshire is one of the key sites in Europe relating to the development of aviation technology and aeronautical research. Its closest comparable site in a European context is Chalais Meudon in France, where a variety of buildings – including an airship hangar of 1884 (the earliest in the world) and wind tunnels – have survived, and the Adlershof research and development centre at Johannisthal to the east of Berlin. A balloon factory and the Royal Engineers' School of Ballooning moved to Farnborough in 1905–06, and the portable airship hangar (re-erected in 2004) remains from a number of dirigible sheds. The first British Army aeroplane was flown from this site in

October 1908, by the American Samuel Cody. The headquarters survives from the Royal Engineers' Air Battalion, founded in 1911, comprising a school building with attached balloon mobilisation store. One hangar (The Black Sheds) survives from the pre-First World War air station. The planning of the R52 wind tunnel building in 1916 marked a critical period in Farnborough's development, for public censure over the vulnerability of the Royal Aircraft Factory's BE2c fighter had led to its closure as a site for the manufacture of aircraft by the British state. Farnborough, renamed the Royal Aircraft Establishment, was now placed at the heart of cutting-edge developments in aviation technology lasting into the jet age. It closed as a research establishment in 1999, and a museum has been established within the premises of the Farnborough Air Sciences Trust (FAST). The site also retains the internationally significant wind tunnels of 1934–35 and 1939–42.

The RAF Museum at Hendon is located on the fomer Hendon aerodrome from which the RNAS conducted the night defence of London. Two of the three paired hangars with Belfast-truss roofs built in 1917 for the Aircraft Acceptance Park at Hendon survive, now joined, reclad and incorporated into the RAF Museum. Also on this site are two contemporary buildings from the Grahame-White aircraft factory. The museum at Montrose is sited within a unique survival of hangars dating from 1913 to 1916.

At Hooton, on the Dee, all three hangars of the 1918 Training Depot Station survive, now in the care of The Hooton Park Trust. These are more altered than the examples at Duxford but their importance is buttressed by its later history and the unique survival of its twin Training Depot Station at North Shotwick (Sealand) in North Wales.

The flying field together with 24 workshop and barracks buildings have survived from the Home Defence station at Stow Maries in Essex, from which aircraft flew in the defence of London from Zeppelins and, after June 1917, Gotha bombers (Fig 5.5). The site has now been purchased by the Stow Maries Aerodrome Trust with the help of grants from English Heritage and the National Heritage Memorial Fund and loans from Maldon District Council and Essex County Council.

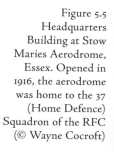

Figure 5.5 Headquarters Building at Stow Maries Aerodrome, Essex. Opened in 1916, the aerodrome was home to the 37 (Home Defence) Squadron of the RFC (© Wayne Cocroft)

Seaplane stations

Important structures remain from coastal stations that played a key role in convoy protection and anti-U-boat operations, including the seaplane hangars at Calshot on the Solent and Mount Batten in Plymouth. At Lee-on-Solent steel-framed hangars survive adjacent to a concrete slipway. The last known seaplane hanger in Scotland, at Stannergate in Dundee, was demolished in the 1980s (Fig 5.6).

Calshot Activity Centre on the Solent makes full use of its unique surviving group of seaplane hangars, which were sited next to one of Henry VIII's coastal forts built in the 1530s in order to help defend shipping in this strategically crucial area. It retains the best-preserved group of early seaplane hangers in Europe, ranging from a small timber hangar built early in 1914 for housing Sopwith Bat Boats to the immense steel-framed hangar, now in use as a sports centre and velodrome, which housed the Felixstowe flying boats used on anti-submarine patrols.

Berehaven, Co Cork was the location of a United States Navy Base which acted as a US air station providing kite balloons for attachment to Royal Navy destroyers, while at nearby White Gate, Lower Aghada, a US Naval Base was established for the operation of the Curtiss flying-boats. The remains of the 1918 pier and entrance gates for the Base can still be seen today.

Figure 5.6 Interior view of the Stannergate seaplane hangar near Dundee. The building was demolished in the 1980s (© RCAHMS)

5.3 Airship stations

Background

At the outbreak of war, when endurance and greater payloads were required, rigid and non-rigid airships appeared to offer many advantages over contemporary flimsy and under-powered aircraft.

By 1914, military airship activity was concentrated at Farnborough, Hampshire, where a government Balloon Factory had been established in 1905. In order to meet this new demand for airships, in 1909 Vickers Sons & Maxim Ltd built an airship assembly shed in the Cavendish dock at Barrow-in-Furness, Cumbria, while c 1910 an airship station was established at Wormwood Scrubs, London; this was later used for the production of the Sea Scout series of balloons. The armaments manufacturer Sir William Beardmore also built an airship assembly building at Inchinnan, Renfrewshire (Fig 5.7). In 1916–17 a Royal Airship Works for the Admiralty was built at Cardington, Bedfordshire, where the enormous hangars still survive (Fig 5.8).

Figure 5.7 The Inchinnan airship shed under construction by the Arrol Company in 1916. The shed measured 213m x 46m and was 30m high (© RCAHMS: Sir William Arrol Collection)

Airship stations

Airship stations are a relatively unusual class of site and just 28 operational stations were built, including three in Ireland and one on the Isle of Man. These comprised twelve airship stations and sixteen sub-stations, or 'mooring out' sites. To afford shelter these were often sited in disused quarries or woodland clearings. The principal activities of these stations were anti-submarine patrol work and convoy patrols. This is reflected in their distribution, with eleven of the stations located close to the south coast, while eight guarded the east coast and a further seven the Irish Sea. The northernmost airship station was at Caldale in Orkney; the northernmost kite balloon station was in Shetland.

Figure 5.8 Aerial
view of the surviving
airship sheds
at Cardington,
Bedfordshire
(© English Heritage)

A typical parent station might comprise two or three airship sheds. In the site's technical area was a hydrogen plant and gas holders to produce and store the gas for filling the balloons. An acetylene generator house was located close by. Other technical buildings were common to conventional airfields including motor transport garages, a wireless hut, stores, workshops, water tower, a coal store, power house to generate electricity, and a magazine to hold bombs and small arms ammunition. In the domestic area was the headquarters building, separate barracks for male and female personnel, a parade ground, canteens, and an officers' mess. The handling of airships was a labour-intensive activity and the largest might require 500 men, while smaller ones required about 100. Kingsnorth, on the Hoo Peninsula, Medway, was one of the largest stations and was home to around 900 personnel.

Airship shed design

At the beginning of the war there were just six airship sheds; by the end of the war this number had increased to 61. A variety of shed designs was used, although all were typically aligned in the direction of the prevailing wind, with wind breaks at either end to prevent sudden gusts of wind knocking the airship against the doors of the shed. At either end of the shed were sliding doors set on rails, although at Kingsnorth circular marks showing on aerial photographs suggest that the doors could be swung open. Sixteen airship sheds were timber-framed and the remainder steel-framed. Most were clad in corrugated iron sheeting and painted in camouflage colours. As airships grew in size so did their ground facilities and at Howden, Norfolk, No 2 shed, built by Sir William Arrol & Co Ltd, was 754ft (230m) long, 410ft (122m) wide and 130ft (40m) high. It was the largest building in the country and used around 5200 tons of steel, the equivalent weight of a naval light cruiser.

Identifying sites

By the end of the war, with the rapid advances in aircraft technology, military interest in airships waned. By September 1919 the majority had been deleted from the inventory of the newly formed Royal Air Force. Over the following decade most airship stations were closed and the airship sheds sold for scrap. A rare survival is the airship shed at Cardington that was used as the home of the ill-fated R101, which was lost with 43 lives in 1930 (see Fig 5.8). Adjacent to it is a second airship shed, relocated from its original base at Pulham, Norfolk. On the Hoo Peninsula the upper sections of one of the sheds from Kingsnorth has been re-erected as a farm building, and at Padstow, Cornwall, sections of a shed from Mullion have been reused as a bus garage. At Farnborough, two sections of pre-war, portable steel-lattice-framed airship shed have recently been reunited. Recent aerial photography (Fig 5.9) has revealed the outlines of the airship station at Milton, Pembrokeshire surviving as parchmarks under the Second World War airfield. At other stations their sites may be traced as concrete floor slabs, as at Lenabo in north-east Scotland, and exceptionally buildings from the technical and domestic sites may survive, adapted to new uses. The best-surviving technical site may be found to the east of Edinburgh at East Fortune airfield, where camp buildings including barracks, messes, offices and a power-generating station remain standing. Four kite balloon stations have been discovered in Scotland; a plan of the one at Lerwick shows twelve canvas hangars but evidence from elsewhere is currently lacking.

At Bentra, near Whitehead in Co Antrim, an airship mooring station was developed to facilitate airships travelling from the main base at Luce Bay, south-east of Stranraer on the Scottish coast, providing safe housing for the balloons in the event of adverse weather conditions. As the war at sea progressed the sub-station became integral in the protection of vessels within the North Channel against attack from German U-boats. In 1915 the site at Bentra became the home of the first military aviation facility in Ireland, from which the RNAS and their airships patrolled the waters between Ireland and Scotland. Other similar locations in Ireland include Ballyliffan RNAS, Co Donegal, a Sub-station to Llangefni, Anglesey 1918–19; Buncrana (Rathmullen, Lough Swilly) RNAS, Co Donegal, which operated a kite balloon detachment; and RNAS Malahide, Co Dublin and Killeagh, Co Cork, both Airship Mooring Stations.

When attempting to research and identify such sites, important factors to consider include the topography of the site and how it reflects its original mission; the type of site – a parent station or sub-station; how the site has been adapted by later uses; and whether the functional areas can still be discerned.

Figure 5.9a Aerial view of RNAS Pembroke shortly after it opened (Courtesy of Deric Brock)

Figure 5.9b RNAS Pembroke (Milton Aerodrome) Air Station: parchmarks showing access roads and footings of hangars and wind-turbulence screens dating from 1915 to 1920, underlying the Second World War runways (© NMRW)

5.4 Anti-aircraft sites

Background

At the outbreak of war powered flight by heavier-than-air machines was just over a decade old. Its potential both for military reconnaissance and attack was quickly recognised and France and Germany rapidly developed both aircraft and airships. Britain was slower to exploit the potential of air power, but the impending threat from the air was recognised and discussed as early as 1909. Opinions about the best ways to counter this menace would be familiar themes in the following decades. Were fixed or mobile anti-aircraft guns, or armed airships and aircraft, more effective? Where would an enemy choose to attack? Would it be the country's major dockyards, ammunition stores and armaments factories, or its major towns and cities?

Location and site types

In August 1913, a meeting was held to discuss the defence of the important ammunition depots at Lodge Hill and Chattenden, Kent, that served the Chatham and Sheerness dockyards. By early 1913 guns were mounted at three sites on timber platforms, and a few months later permanent sites were in place. By the outbreak of war anti-aircraft guns were in place at Portsmouth, Barrow, the Tyne, and in London on the roofs of a handful of public buildings. Elsewhere, ad hoc arrangements were made for the protection of key installations, such as dockyards, magazines, and munitions factories.

Relatively little research has been carried out on First World War anti-aircraft sites. For many of these sites information is lacking on their precise location and also on the layout of individual sites. Given that this was a new technology using a variety of guns, considerable variability of site layouts might be expected. The Lodge Hill battery at Chattenden, Kent, is diamond-shaped and comprises an infantry blockhouse, a store and officers' quarters, defensive barracks, and two concrete footings for the guns; the whole site was originally surrounded by a barbed-wire fence. At King's Cross, London, the main anti-aircraft gun was set on a raised timber platform, while a lighter gun was positioned at ground level. Ancillary features included a sentry box, an accommodation hut, stores, and a flag staff surrounded by white-painted stones or bricks. The Great War Archaeology Group has undertaken research on the First Blitz and London's air defences. At Monkham's Hall, near Waltham Abbey, Essex, excavation of an anti-aircraft site revealed a concrete platform 8m square with a polygonal projection, at the centre of which was a single gun mounting and to the rear two brick shelters.

At the Armistice in November 1918 there were 48 areas defended against air attack, stretching from Gretna on the Scottish border to Plymouth in the south-west. By 1920, almost the entire air defence system had been dismantled and remaining expertise was restricted to the army's small school of anti-aircraft defence.

London Air Defence Area

One response to the attacks by German aircraft was the London Air Defence Area (LADA), established 31 July 1917. This was the world's first integrated air defence system: zones were established for the anti-aircraft guns and between these, patrol lines for the fighters. A control and communication system was set up, with reports of raiders telephoned to a control centre in the Admiralty. From this control centre the War Office, Speaker of the House of Commons, the railway companies, gun sites and fighter airfields were informed about the enemy approach. Other features included three screens of tethered balloons, acetylene searchlights, and semi-mobile sound locators. By November 1918, London's defences comprised 286 guns, 387 searchlights and eight Home Defence fighter squadrons, representing about 200 aircraft. The new technology of wireless voice communication was also applied to the directing of fighters towards their quarries. Ten aerodromes and airship stations were also identified for anti-aircraft defences, although it is unclear if any were emplaced. In addition to the fixed gun sites, mobile guns were set on motor wagons.

Early warning

For the system to function most efficiently the guns and fighters required advanced warning of an attack. At first reports were made by telephone to the control centre by police officers, military units, and even railway employees. In the absence of a telephone, reports were sent by telegram. This simple visual reporting system was later supplemented by sound locators – large funnels or dishes used to focus the noise of aero-engines. The London system was based on mobile equipment, while on the coast large concrete sound mirrors were constructed to detect raiders as they crossed the sea.

Figure 5.10 Reconstruction painting by Peter Dunn of the Lodge Hill Anti-aircraft Battery (© English Heritage)

Figure 5.11 The recently uncovered acoustic mirrors at Fan Bay, near Dover. The 15′ mirror on the right was installed in 1917; the larger one dates from the 1920s (© National Trust)

Key sites

The Lodge Hill battery at Chattenden, Kent, completed in 1913, is a remarkable survival and is probably the world's oldest surviving anti-aircraft site (Fig 5.10). Close by is another contemporary site at Beacon Hill, but this is less well-preserved. Only about eleven acoustic sound mirrors were constructed and as a result survivals are very rare. Along the north-east coast, four of the six wartime mirrors survive, while three survive in Kent including two recently re-excavated examples at Fan Bay (Fig 5.11). At Selsey, West Sussex, another one remains incorporated into a house.

5.5 Air raids

At 11am on Christmas Eve 1914 Lieutenant Von Prondsynski, flying a Taube monoplane, dropped a bomb in the garden of Castlemount Court, Taswell Street, Dover, the first aerial bomb dropped on England. Over the following years a total of 111 raids by German airships and aircraft were launched against Britain, resulting in around 1500 deaths and 3300 injuries.

Airship raids

The first German Zeppelin airship raid occurred on 19 January 1915, when bombs were dropped on Great Yarmouth, King's Lynn and other east coast towns. London was the principal target, although with their great range airships travelled widely, sometimes carried off course by adverse winds (Fig 5.12). In north-west England an arc of towns between Halifax and Liverpool was attacked.

In the Midlands an airship was seen over Shrewsbury and bombs were dropped on Dudley. On the night of 2/3 April 1916 two Zeppelins reached the Forth; unable to identify targets at the Rosyth naval base, they bombed Edinburgh and Leith, killing twelve people. They are said to have encountered 'desultory machine-gun fire' from the anti-invasion defences south of Arthur's Seat, in the Royal Park. As a consequence of this raid, the Home Defence network of fighter squadrons and airfields was extended to the Forth. Similarly, War Office maps and plans from this time start to record 'Anti-Aircraft Guns', often at coast defence batteries, demonstrating the value of such documents in tracing the history of these installations.

Figure 5.12 A postcard image of an air raid on London, 13 October 1915 (Courtesy of Wayne Cocroft)

In total ten airships and 22 aircraft were brought down by the air defences. Archaeological excavation of two Zeppelin crash sites revealed few artefacts, a reflection of the relatively flimsy construction of these vessels and low impact speeds. A similar pattern might also be expected with First World War aircraft crash sites. During the war a total of 202 airship sorties were mounted against Britain, resulting in 557 deaths.

Aircraft raids

As the country's air defences improved, especially after May 1917, large twin-engined Gotha and later Giant aircraft were more commonly used. The majority of the German aircraft were based in Belgium and London was their prime target, although many of the bombs intended for the capital fell in the neighbouring counties.

Air raid shelters

As the war progressed the indiscriminate nature of the air attacks had an increasingly adverse affect on civilian morale; in the east of London it was cited as the cause of a large drop in industrial productivity. The attacks also tied down both personnel and resources. As described above, London was ringed with air defence fighter airfields, searchlights, balloons with dangling wire aprons and anti-aircraft guns. However, the government decided against a campaign of mass public shelter construction; instead it encouraged the use of substantial basements and in London underground stations were used as shelters and first aid centres. The arches beneath Bishopsgate goods station provided one such shelter and on 28 January 1918 it was the scene of a

Figure 5.13 A rare example of purpose-built air-raid shelters at the Royal Gunpowder Factory, Waltham Abbey, Essex (Courtesy of Royal Gun Powder Mills)

tragic loss of life when fourteen people were crushed to death by a crowd terrified by a warning maroon. The same night 38 were killed by a direct hit on a shelter at Long Acre, near Covent Garden. In north London the arches of Edmonton Green railway viaduct were identified as a shelter and in Dover, caves were used. Examples of purpose-built shelters are rare, but one set of sand-bag shelters is pictured at the Royal Gunpowder Factory, Waltham Abbey, Essex (Fig 5.13). Elsewhere railway companies built 'dug outs' from railway sleepers and sandbags for essential staff. A surviving First World War air raid shelter has yet to be identified. Ad hoc shelters are known to have existed in the cellars beneath both Liverpool Street Station and the adjacent Great Eastern Hotel, and Waterloo Station.

Traces

Today traces of this campaign may be detected as shrapnel scars on walls or 'new' houses and other buildings constructed to replace those lost to bombing. In London there are many traces of the air raids, including shrapnel damage to the Sphinx statue and Cleopatra's Needle on the Thames embankment, and at Lincoln's Inn. On the side of the Leeds & Liverpool canal at Wigan, a crater caused by a Zeppelin bomb survived at least into the 1990s. Few of these sites have been located precisely and many would benefit from further research. Elsewhere, the sites of aerial attacks may be marked by plaques and other memorials (see Fig 1.9), while in towns attacked from the air, such as Margate and Sheerness, civilians who lost their lives are commemorated on local war memorials.

These early wartime air raid precautions are an under-researched topic and investigations in council and other records may reveal local organisations, shelters and first aid centres. A variety of sources can provide clues, including historic photographs, shrapnel scars (documentary evidence will be needed to confirm their date), gaps or changes in building styles, and the records of public buildings utilised as shelters.

CHAPTER 6

Commemoration

6.1 Introduction

The physical evidence relating to the commemoration of the First World War is most familiar to the modern observer in the form of the war memorials found across the UK, although other forms of memorial exist. The commemoration of the war dead in the Great War was part of a steadily developing tradition, the earliest recorded being that for the 7th-century Battle of Dunnichen. Up until the Victorian era memorials were generally erected for the Officer class, those whose families and friends back home had funds to subscribe to monuments or plaques. For major national heroes the wider public contributed but there were rarely memorials to the rank and file. This began to change with the Crimean War and in the aftermath of the Indian Mutiny and particularly the Second Anglo-Boer War of 1899–1902. Unlike these memorials, which were frequently erected at the behest of local leaders, 'Great War' memorials were generally (ostensibly at least) community-driven efforts. Experience shows, however, that the members of the committees who presided over the creation of these memorials were often local dignitaries, clerics and landowners.

War memorials are present in public areas, like parks and communal urban spaces, as well as semi-public/private locations such as workplaces, churches, schools and sporting arenas. They record the names of the dead, and, in some cases, those who served. Whilst it is often thought that commemoration of the conflict mainly took place in the inter-war period, research is increasingly demonstrating that these mechanisms of remembrance originate during the war itself; memorials in Britain were erected from at least as early as 1915.

This date is significant, for after 1915 the British government decreed that service personnel killed as the result of the conflict would no longer be repatriated (prior to this, it seems, it was possible for families to bring their dead home, at their own expense). What this domestically controversial move meant was that any treatment afforded to the dead, their burial and the form of material commemoration, was in the hands of the state.

Thus the comfort of a known burial and a grave to visit was denied to the next of kin, although arguably this was not intended to be the case. Both during the war and afterwards, the task of commemorating the dead at the various theatres of war was officially the responsibility of the Graves Registration Unit (GRU) (later the Imperial War Graves Commission – IWGC). Families were supplied with photographs of battlefield graves and many took up the opportunity in the inter-war years to visit. The Commission was to take responsibility for the design and construction of the cemeteries and memorials to the dead at the various fronts, in order to assuage concerns at an official level that the families of the dead might erect private battlefield memorials that could be considered 'inappropriate'.

The earliest form of commemoration as the numbers of dead mounted during the war was Rolls of Honour/Service; lists of names of the dead and those serving. Individual and temporary memorials also proliferated during the conflict. Some communities, particularly in working-class districts, began to erect relatively cheap, temporary shrines made of wood and paper based around small-scale localities, such as streets. While such shrines were, in part, a spontaneous response to the conflict, they were also encouraged by certain Anglo-Catholic ministers.

Figure 6.1 An image published in the *Illustrated London News* of Queen Mary visiting a street shrine (Courtesy of Jonathan Trigg)

The shrines were used to hold offerings of flowers and formed stopping points for pilgrimages around a parish, at which services and more informal prayers were held. The strong Catholic overtones drew criticism from parts of the Anglican Church and only after campaigns in the national newspapers and by the Lord Mayor of London, together with the effect of a well-publicised visit by Queen Mary to the shrines (Fig 6.1), did they become more acceptable. Few of these original shrines remain; some were replaced by more formal examples and in some cases they were supplanted by permanent examples at the end of the war (Fig 6.2).

At a governmental level, plans were commissioned in 1917 for a National, later Imperial War Museum to commemorate the conflict. Furthermore, in August 1918 a large temporary wooden memorial was erected in Hyde Park, London, unveiled on the fourth anniversary of the declaration of war (throughout the war, 4 August was treated as a national day of remembrance). Over 100,000 people were said to have visited the shrine in the first week and it remained open for over a year.

At home, however, there was less of an official presence (with the exception of commemorating those who had died on British soil), and thus local communities and families could take the initiative in finding a way to commemorate those that had served and, more importantly, those that would never return. The erection of the temporary shrine in Hyde Park certainly prompted debate about the nature of future, more permanent, memorials and it was this process that led to the construction of the plethora of war memorials that we see today.

Each memorial is the result of a varying set of processes, and thus has its own narrative, ranging from those who initiated and legislated on the memorial design, the means of fund-raising and location, to the choice of sculptor. Voluntary subscription was considered the most suitable form of raising funds in the commemorative process. Whether pro-active fundraising was appropriate was in some cases a divisive issue. Furthermore, different memorials were erected at varying costs, and it is not always the most obvious communities that paid the greatest amount.

By way of contrast, based on populations in 1921, Glasgow communities raised around £104,000 for the erection of a memorial for the city; Leeds, which had half the population raised merely £6000. The 53,000 people of Barnsley raised around £3000 and the district of Hoylake and West Kirkby, with a population of 17,000, raised nearly £8000. Funding as a whole was a serious issue, with proposals for the Imperial War Museum being downsized as the result of a lack of funds.

Commemoration, therefore, had an economic impact. Stone masons provided large numbers of mass-produced designs and provided large amounts of cheap material, advertising, for example, through the medium of specialised catalogues. Professional architects were responsible for the majority of the specially commissioned sculptures, making use of their professional organisations;

Figure 6.2 A preserved street shrine in Eton Street, Hull; a larger example can be seen in Sharp Street in the city, but such memorials are now rare. Among the names listed are some from the Royal Naval Reserve Trawler division (© Tegwen Roberts)

sculptors argued that their work was superior to that of the architects, but received far fewer commissions. There was particular concern at the stereotyped designs produced and numerous bodies, such as the Royal Academy of Arts and Church of England, produced guidelines, while the Civic Arts Association was specifically formed for this purpose. The most well-known design is the 'Cross of Sacrifice', by Sir Reginald Blomfield (see Fig 1.4).

As noted, the memorials erected in Britain to the First World War were primarily the result of the efforts of local community leaders and civic groups who formed memorial committees, with relatively little, or more often no, central state involvement. The British War Memorials Committee, a national foundation created by Lord Beaverbrook when he became Minister of Information in February 1917, focused on limited projects rather than trying to initiate a national response.

In general, the committees were chaired by local dignitaries, such as town mayors and councillors, who then brought in a wider range of society, although this 'democratisation' of the committee membership was far from universal. The inclusion of Christian elements in the memorials and associated ceremonies could exclude minority religious groups. Veterans of the conflict frequently considered themselves excluded from the process and there were numerous complaints that the wealthier members of society were given a disproportionate role. In the political arena, Unionists in Northern Ireland made the commemorative process a key element, emphasising their role in important actions such as the Battle of the Somme.

Commemoration was not limited to memorials without any utilitarian or social function: numerous examples can be found of buildings and parks and gardens. In addition to their name, many of these also incorporated a memorial in the form of a plaque or Roll of Honour.

6.2 War memorials and cemeteries

War memorials, found in almost every community across the UK, take a range of forms from the perceived traditional cross, cenotaph or plaque to the more unusual stained glass windows, park benches, lychgates, buildings (hospitals, halls and homes), gardens or church fittings. Each community, or family in the case of memorials to individuals, responded differently and war memorial heritage is a rich, diverse and fascinating topic as a result. Even the communities who erected memorials vary; whilst geographical ones are often a focal point for village or town ceremonies on Remembrance Day, churches, schools, workplaces and youth groups as well as individual families also commemorated those they had lost. Given the range and scope of war memorials, this section will deal with those memorials which are primarily war memorials – objects which have no wider utilitarian or social purposes as compared to the open spaces, halls and homes that are dealt with in subsequent sections.

Of the estimated 100,000 war memorials, the First World War is associated with around two thirds. Across the nation the emotion and grief following that conflict was reflected in an unprecedented programme of memorialisation. The sheer numbers who died meant there would be many more memorials than those for the Crimean and Boer wars but there were also further differences as many communities chose to remember those who served as well as those who fell and even the 'Thankful' villages, who lost no one, sought to record that fact with monuments of thanks at having survived unscathed as a community. As these memorials are community-based they are overwhelmingly accessible. They are often central features in our towns and villages or in civic or community buildings such as Town Halls, churches or schools. Those that are now the most challenging to access are often the workplace memorials in commercial premises where arrangements are necessary to visit, or memorials in former churches or chapels which have been converted. In some circumstances memorials had to remain *in situ*, even if inside, making them difficult to visit and record.

People did not wait until the end of the First World War to commemorate the war dead. Memorials began to be erected during the conflict although these tended to be focused on individuals. Once the conflict was over, communities responded by working together to raise funds, determine design and erect their own memorials. Memorials for the First World War are rarely combined with earlier monuments (as many communities chose to do after 1945). They were therefore new features in villages, towns and cities and can be a key source of information about the communities at that time. Occasionally they took precedence, as in the case of the Loyal North Lancashire Regiment in Preston, Lancashire where the Boer War memorial was moved into Aveham Park in order for the First World War memorial to be erected where it had stood in the Market Place. Some communities felt so strongly that multiple memorials were erected. One example is the village of Datchet, Berkshire which has a calvary erected in 1919 on London Road, a wheel cross known as 'The Women's Memorial' erected in the churchyard in 1920, an obelisk erected on the green in 1920 (funded by community donations of £600), and a Roll of Honour in the church. The multiplicity may be due to different purposes for the memorials or the desire of members of the community to commemorate in different ways. Making sure there is a record of these different forms is vital to ensure that the varied means of memorialisation are recognised and this can lead to further research into why there was variety, enabling the physical remains to influence our understanding of society at that time.

In contrast to earlier practices, memorials were largely built in busy, public spaces. The importance of these memorials is that people whose loved ones lay overseas had a place to focus their mourning: the memorials became surrogate graves and sacred spaces.

As well as the increase in numbers and variety of forms of war memorial, an additional change occasioned by the Great War in military commemoration was the nomination of certain days in the calendar, such as Armistice Day, for annual ceremonies. After the war, the date of the focus of remembrance switched from 4 August to 11 November to mark the anniversary of the Armistice, or Armisticetide as it was originally designated. Ceremonies, including the two-minute silence, became the norm, with the Cenotaph becoming the hub for these events. Such occasions were equated to religious festivals. As well as the usual press coverage, the national ceremonies were also broadcast on the radio from 1928.

Types of memorial

The simplest form of memorial was the Roll of Honour/Service, providing a list of the dead. While these are typically civic memorials, they are also found in parish churches, where frequently they list all those who served, as well as the dead whose names are recorded on the local memorial. In some cases books were created, especially in locations where the number of dead were so numerous as to make their recording on memorials unfeasible. In many cases, the military rank of the dead was omitted, creating the impression of equality in death.

Obelisks and plaques were particularly popular choices for memorials, along with Celtic crosses in Scotland, Ireland and Wales (which also appealed to Christian heritage), as they were relatively cheap to build and fitted in with existing civic architecture. Where servicemen were represented, they tended to be ordinary soldiers, sailors and airmen, in contrast to the earlier practice of representing heroic officers. In many cases, they can be seen to be raising their helmets or rifles in a sign of victory, a style which seems to have its roots in memorials to the Second Anglo-Boer War. Monuments which were classically inspired often came in for criticism for being over-ornate.

Many memorials harked back to a medieval past. Memorial windows which featured knights on horseback were juxtaposed with more modern weaponry, such as tanks, aircraft and artillery. The image of Saint George, frequently represented in armour and on horseback, was often employed in England (Fig 6.3). In Wales, the war memorial at Miskin is designed as a medieval cross, but figures of service

Figure 6.3 The image of St George was a popular choice for memorials; this one is at Colchester, Essex (© Jonathan Trigg)

personnel are included instead of religious figures, while that at Rhayader includes a pronounced patriotic message where a sculptural group depicts a Welsh dragon defeating a German eagle. The Scottish National War Memorial is a Scots Baronial-style hall designed by Lorimer, which attempts to fit in with its historic surroundings in Edinburgh Castle. Northern Ireland's main war memorial is the Belfast Cenotaph, with a Garden of Remembrance situated alongside. The memorial is located in the grounds of Belfast City Hall at Donegal Square West and is a fine example of commemoration within Ulster where it is has come to be regarded as a symbol of victory and honour. The Island Bridge National War Memorial Gardens in Dublin, designed by Sir Edwin Lutyens, are dedicated to the 49,400 Irish soldiers who gave their lives during the Great War 1914–18.

In addition to the Cenotaph as a national, albeit empty, memorial, the government also organised the creation of the Tomb of the Unknown Warrior as a national war grave. The idea had begun to gain support towards the end of the war, and was actively promoted by some British veterans groups in 1919. However, as with the construction of the Cenotaph, it was originally viewed with some disquiet, as a second site was considered unnecessary. Nevertheless, following lobbying, particularly by the cleric and former Forces chaplain David Railton, the Tomb was likewise unveiled on Armistice Day, 1920.

The Cenotaph and Tomb of the Unknown Warrior reference the nation's war dead as a whole, but hold a particular resonance for the dead for whom no known resting place has yet been discovered.

Other items that were selected as memorials included church furniture, such as sponsored lecterns, bells and screens – these tend to be the preserve of individual or family memorialisation. There are also 'utilitarian' war memorials, which take the form of halls, parks, clock towers, gates, hospitals and so forth dedicated to the memory of the conflict. Even large-scale urban redevelopments were proposed, such as the rebuilding of the centre of Westminster as essentially a large memorial complex. There were debates on which types of memorial were considered most appropriate, spurred on by the formation of both local and national societies promoting various viewpoints.

At the time of writing, the IWM's War Memorials Archive lists approximately 43,000 memorials related to the First World War. This number is likely to be an underestimation, given that a number of memorials have been lost for a variety of reasons; there are those that are yet to be recorded, and still more that are being erected to the conflict in the present day. War Memorials Online, seeking to create a greater understanding of the condition of war memorials, suggests about two thirds of war memorials in the UK have a First World War connection. Further public contributions are needed to help indentify the condition of them all.

87 · WHITEHALL AND THE CENOTAPH, LONDON.

The Cenotaph

The Cenotaph, in Whitehall, London, became an inspiration for similar memorials unveiled throughout the country (Fig 6.4). This was originally a temporary wooden memorial, instigated at the behest of David Lloyd George and the Peace Celebrations Committee in mid-1919 as the focus of a victory march through Whitehall; as with the street shrines, this also became a focus of anti-Catholic criticism. However the memorial was constructed and was found to be very popular, with 500,000 people estimated to have visited it in the first four days. As a result the memorial was left *in situ* for over a year, with many more making the pilgrimage to the site. The longer than expected period of use meant it soon became dilapidated and discussion followed on what to do with the site. There was concern from government ministers that a permanent memorial might be vandalised, while the press were opposed to the removal of the existing monument. In the end, Edwin Lutyens was commissioned to create a new, permanent memorial which was unveiled on Armistice Day, 1920. In November of that year, it was visited by over a million people.

Figure 6.4 A postcard of the Cenotaph in Whitehall, London in 1929 (Courtesy of Wayne Cocroft)

Cemeteries

Distinct from war memorials, the graves of those deemed casualties of the First World War are managed by the Commonwealth War Graves Commission (CWGC). The CGWC is funded by the partner governments of the Commonwealth nations and has a statutory responsibility to protect and care for these sites. What is often not realised is the sheer scale of its work in the United Kingdom. It is the country with the second highest number of people commemorated within its borders, with 12,341 different burial sites managed by the Commission across the country. The largest number are commemorated in France, with Belgium third. The United Kingdom sites vary, with large cemeteries such as Brookwood, Surrey (where 5072 identified casualties lie) holding numerous graves alongside the cross of sacrifice and cenotaph. Elsewhere, a small group of headstones may be located within a cemetery, while some are single graves such as that of Private L Longbottom who died on 30 April 1918 and is buried at St Peter's in Bishopton, Durham. In some cases men may have returned home with injuries and subsequently died meaning they were buried in their local cemetery by the family but the family chose to have a Commission headstone (then or subsequently), ensuring the Commission have a responsibility for tending the site. Through the centenary, which includes their own founding in 1917, the CWGC is seeking to raise awareness of its UK sites and further information on this, the sites and its wider work can be found on the Commission's website.

6.3 Village halls

Before the 19th century many villages did not have a public meeting space outside of their religious buildings. At this time, the Church and Chapel were an important part of the local community and their roles often included schooling children or hosting public meetings. However, in the Victorian period religious views changed and churches were thought of more as a 'sacred' space, which meant that secular activities had to 'stop at the door' and pews were reintroduced to naves. This reduced the ability of the community to use the space for other activities, and while some had access to 'church rooms' or 'parish rooms', even where these were separate from the church itself there were restrictions on what sort of activities could take place in the building.

From around 1850 to 1914, there were reports about increasing rates of alcoholism in rural areas and worries that lots of people were leaving the countryside for towns. In response to this, a number of Village Reading Rooms and Institutes were built in the 19th century, usually by a local landowner, clergyman or company.

Reading Rooms were small, housing such activities as billiards, bagatelle and the reading of illustrated newspapers and books, but they could not accommodate events needing space, like dances, plays or film shows. Many of these buildings were only open at certain times of the day, and these could change according to the season or work patterns. They catered almost entirely for men and were often governed by regulations imposed by the clergy or benefactor. These buildings typically had a large oblong room used as a general reading room, although sometimes there were smaller rooms opening from it, to let separate activities take place. At the same time, 'Village Rooms' and 'Village Clubs' or 'Institutes' were also being constructed by wealthy benefactors, sometimes as a memorial to an individual or family, or as the commemoration of a national event, such as Queen Victoria's Diamond Jubilee in 1897/8. In architectural terms, many of these new buildings follow a 'picturesque' style of village architecture, as can be seen in the books of contemporary architectural writers of the mid-19th century, such as P F Robinson and J C Loudon. They also fit with a heightened sense of paternalism and a growing desire amongst the rich – especially those with 'new money' generated by the industrial growth of Britain – to create new and impressive 'estates'.

The First World War was the catalyst for social change in the British countryside, and Village Clubs and Halls were at the heart of this. During the war the lives of rural working-class men and women had changed profoundly – the men went off to war and mixed with city dwellers, men of different social standing with a less-deferential attitude to their 'betters', and trade union members. Women had similar mind-broadening experiences in munitions factories and other war work. 'Hut Life' had been established behind the lines

Figure 6.5 Acaster Malbis Memorial Institute, near York. Opened in 1927, the hall was built of locally made bricks and was paid for by subscriptions. Donors names are recorded on the plaques: £10 for a large one, £5 for a small one (© Catrina Appleby)

in France where recreational facilities were provided by the YMCA and the Church Army, and this developed into more sophisticated entertainment such as concerts, lectures, and educational classes, all of which were organised by the men themselves. The de-mobbed men took these experiences back to the villages, where they questioned the 'old rule' of their community by the gentry and clerics.

This change in attitude, combined with a national desire to provide memorials to those who had served in the war and lots of surplus War Department huts, saw an explosion in the numbers of Village and Memorial Halls during the 1920s. Many of the returning soldiers felt that a 'Memorial Hall' would be the most fitting tribute to those that had lost their lives in the war, and also to those that had served and survived (Fig 6.5). As many villages were keen to establish a hall as quickly as possible, the largest ex-servicemen's organisation, 'Comrades of the Great War', asked the government to allow the sale of former army huts at a discount price to ex-servicemen's organisations for use as a social amenity. Similarly, the National Federation of Women's Institutes (NFWI) and the British Legion bought huts and often employed the labour of their own members to erect them. In some cases, private individuals also took action – the wife of the chief commandant of the Church Army in France acquired a redundant Church Army hut for the use of the returning men and had it placed on land close to the centre of the village of Slinfold, Sussex as a memorial to her husband. Some of these new halls became specifically known as the Memorial – or Victory – Hall and a feature of many halls of this period is a plaque commemorating those from the local community who had served and returned, as well as those who had died. The 'Memo' is a particular characteristic of remembrance in Wales.

Layout

The types of rooms found in village halls, their design and function, and indeed how these became used in later years, provide an interesting commentary on changing times. Although such halls are generally characterised by a large hall, incorporating a space for a stage and often with other facilities such as club rooms, kitchens, toilets and cloakrooms, the requirements of villages have changed over time, as have the sort of activities that the halls are used for. Before and following the First World War, and with a very active Boy Scout movement, many halls may have included a room specifically designed to house a rifle range. Billiards was also a popular pastime in the early 20th century, and required a large room of particular dimensions to house the table.

In the 1920s, a typical hall might include:
  + A stage or platform with storage beneath, with perhaps an open fireplace at the rear so that the space could also be used as a lounge;
  + Cloakrooms inside the main entrance porch. Simple coat hooks in the smallest halls but rooms with WC or chemical toilet in the larger halls;
  + A kitchen with a sink and an oil, gas, or coke stove near the stage so that it could double-up as a dressing room;
  + A separate committee/dressing room for a larger hall;

- A billiard room, which needed to be at least 25ft by 18ft (7.6 x 5.4m) to house a full-sized table;
- A Cinematograph – travelling cinemas could set up inside the main hall but a permanent projector room could be incorporated over the entrance porch and cloakrooms. It needed to be built of fireproof materials, be vented to the open air, and be accessible without entering the hall.

In older halls, the original layout may still be identifiable in the plan form, even where rooms such as boiler rooms and coal stores have been converted to other uses. In some cases, original cast-iron radiator systems might still be in use today, although with a renewed boiler, and there could be some evidence for the old stove and chimney.

Some village halls have unusual features that relate to their original use, such as a belfry from an old school or an old fireplace, or have some form of decoration that was paid for by the community or a wealthy benefactor.

During the Second World War, many village halls were used as part of the war effort, providing emergency services to the local population by, for example, adapting them to become a 'school feeding centre'. They were also used extensively for holding fundraising events, tea parties for servicemen on leave, and were an important part of the Victory celebrations.

After the war, whilst more halls continued to be built, there were major shortages, of both people and funds, which continued for many years. New 'modern' materials started to be used for building, including asbestos and concrete, sometimes instead of the more traditional brick and stone. Consequently, some communities still continued to opt for an old army hut – as a 'temporary' measure – and a few of these are still in use today.

6.4 Parks and gardens

As already noted, parks, gardens, playing fields and avenues of trees were another category of living or useful memorials. Often it was ex-servicemen who promoted memorials of this sort which, instead of focusing on the dead, would serve the needs of the living, especially the young. Memorial parks and gardens offered, in the words of one dedicatory speech, a place where 'all people, young and old, could enjoy the beauties of nature in lovely surroundings, near to the centre of the town'.

More research remains to be done on memorial parks and gardens as a type, and they have received surprisingly little notice in either the literature of war memorials, or in surveys of 20th-century landscape and garden design. But a recent preliminary survey has shown that while their geographical spread is wide, it is restricted to areas where land, unless gifted, was available for purchase. Few memorial parks were laid out in older urban areas where land was short, and larger towns and cities often favoured instead substantial building projects

Figure 6.6 Opened in 1921, Rowntree Park in York was the gift of Joseph Rowntree in memory of the 200 workers from the chocolate factory who died (© Catrina Appleby)

such as a museum or hospital as a war memorial. Memorial parks are generally, though not always, modest in terms of design and materials and were often laid out by the borough surveyor working with a local nursery. However, that in no way diminishes their local significance, commissioned as they were as a place's principal war memorial to the fallen. Numbers are still unclear: there are currently 339 gardens and 212 parks or playing fields listed on the Imperial War Museum War Memorials Archive, but it appears likely that there are still more to be recorded. Parks & Gardens UK is currently developing a national gazetteer.

At a national level, Fleetwood Memorial Park in Lancashire and Coventry War Memorial Park are both included on the Historic England *Register of Parks and Gardens of Special Historic Interest* at Grade II, as is Rowntree Park, York, which was originally dedicated as a memorial park after the First World War (Fig 6.6). The imposing neo-classical Welsh National War Memorial forms the centrepiece to Alexandra Gardens in Cathays Park, Cardiff. It is listed as Grade II on the Cadw/ICOMOS Register of Landscapes, Parks and Gardens of Special Historic Interest in Wales, and the park also incorporates war memorials to the fallen in the Spanish Civil War and the Falklands War.

6.5 Homes fit for Heroes

'Good houses, adequate in size, equipment and amenities, to afford satisfactory dwellings for a workingman's family'

Homes fit for Heroes may be defined as housing built under the 1919 Housing and Town Planning Act – known as the Addison Act after the Minister of Health who promoted it – which required local authorities to submit schemes which on approval would be built with a government subsidy and managed by the local authority. As all authorities were required to survey their housing needs, proposals were submitted by Rural and Urban Districts as well as large municipalities, averaging 22 houses for a Rural District to 350 in a County Borough, with 8773 schemes approved by the end of 1920.

Named after Lloyd George's 1918 election campaign slogan, this programme had a pedigree in housing reform from the late 19th century, tackling disease, overcrowding and immorality through slum clearance. A serious pre-war shortage of affordable housing had been exacerbated to produce a shortfall in working-class housing, estimated variously at 300,000 to 500,000 homes (125,000 to 250,000 in Scotland), with the problem worsening as demobilised soldiers married and sought homes in which to bring up their families.

The nation was seen by many to owe a moral debt to those who had suffered, while the political will which drove legislation reflected a range of concerns. A new generation had to be raised which would be physically fit enough to defend the Empire; revolution and Bolshevism were to be deflected (housing already being identified as a key issue for the Home Front in 1917 by the Commission on Industrial Unrest); whilst an additional eight million women voters raised the profile of domestic issues. Other contemporary factors converged to inform the Act. Wartime building by the Ministry of Munitions (see Chapter 3) had provided housing prototypes, whilst the Tudor Walters Report included drawings by Raymond Unwin (responsible for Letchworth First Garden City) which reappeared in the Manual to accompany the Act. Most revolutionary was the state's acceptance of responsibility, but the subsidy and insistence on quality were soon whittled away in a changing economic climate, so that Homes fit for Heroes were built only between 1919 and 1921, with schemes finally completed during 1923–24, reaching a total of 170,090 houses (25,100 in Scotland).

Characteristics

The new estates were generally built on peripheral sites where authorities were able to purchase land. They were expected to be healthy, served by public transport, and in reach of employment. Layout was at a density of twelve houses to the acre which allowed for individual gardens, allotments, open green spaces and playgrounds. Main roads were few and cul-de-sacs were popular. The aspect of the houses was important in order to let in maximum sunlight, avoiding the evils of dark courts and back-to-backs, and this might result in an unusual arrangement

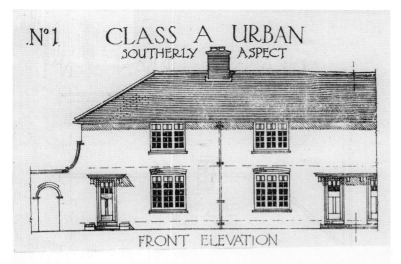

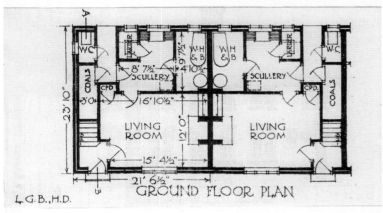

FRONT ELEVATION

GROUND FLOOR PLAN

L.G.B.,H.D.

Figure 6.7 Front elevation and ground-floor plan for a south-facing, non-parlour, three-bedroom house of 10,911 cu ft, from the *Manual for State-Aided Housing Schemes, Local Government Board, 1919* (Courtesy of Helen Caffrey)

of windows, offering a present clue to origin. Shops and public buildings including schools were integral to the scheme.

The houses on these 'cottage estates' might be semi-detached or in groups of four. These could be unified (but not monotonous) within the street view by the use of interlinking screen walls and in some cases were dignified by the use of distinctive set-back corner groups. Simplicity of design was favoured, in a basic neo-Georgian rather than local vernacular. Superficial ornamentation and dormers were avoided, so as to focus on speed of construction and convenience of maintenance, using economies of mass production in doors and windows while achieving new standards internally. Houses generally had three bedrooms over a kitchen/living room of a minimum 180 sq ft (16.7m²), scullery, cool larder, fixed bath (preferably in a separate bathroom), WC and coal store, while 'parlour houses' had an additional room of 120 sq ft (11.1m²), allowing separation of kitchen activities from general living space. A modern heating system also provided hot water. Several designs were offered in the Manual as models and many authorities were happy to use them without alteration (Fig 6.7).

Model Schemes

The magnitude of the programme ensures the likelihood of many schemes awaiting recognition around the country. The following examples indicate some of their diversity. In London, the borough of Poplar had its Chapel House Street Estate designed and built by the Office of Works between October 1919 and 1921, calling it their 'garden city' for its 'quiet, almost villagey atmosphere', but plans for more were reduced in scope and quality by changes in government policy. In the mining and agricultural County Durham, where housing was often tied to employment, 7000 Homes fit for Heroes were built, often in small estates and mostly in areas of thriving mining activity.

Leeds built 3329 houses under the Act, over half of them as parlour houses, in a city where seven out of ten houses were back-to-backs and density could be as high as 70 to the acre. The council appointed its own advisory architect and sent the committee on a fact-finding tour including New Earswick (Parker and Unwin for Rowntree) and Gretna and Well Hall (Ministry of Munitions). A few early examples at Hawksworth used stone facing to reflect local style, but most were simpler in appearance if more adventurous technically, utilising experimental materials such as 'Waller' panelled concrete at Cross Gates (Fig 6.8).

Bristol purchased land extensively on the city outskirts, appointed an architect specifically to work on the new estates, and employed direct labour, raising its initial target of 2000 houses to 5000 with the prospect of government subsidy and issue of bonds. St John's Lane, Bedminster has some substantial semi-detached houses and has retained some of the characteristic screen walls and street corner layouts, while the hipped roofs persist into the estate beyond. Knowle Park also employs interesting rooflines, indicating that individual architectural trademarks may be identified within overall legislative parameters. A broad avenue with adjacent park bounds one side of the estate, which includes church, school (formerly) and shops, with distant green hills supplying the recommended 'beauty of vista' (Fig 6.9). Wellgarth Walk, a cul-de-sac, is composed of semis with notably long frontages but shallow depth, set in generous gardens, and terminates in a group of four with central passage.

Figure 6.8 Experimental 'Waller' panelled concrete houses under construction at Cross Gates Estate, Leeds, 1921 (Reproduced by kind permission of Leeds Library and Information Service)

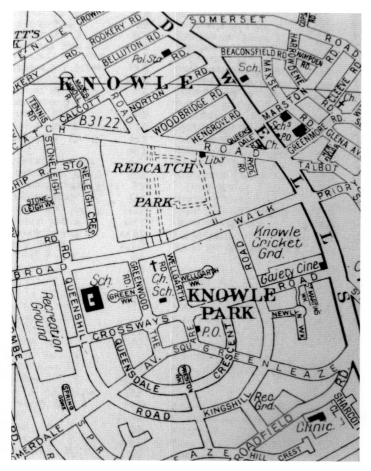

In Ireland, a housing scheme introduced in 1920 proposed that up to 7600 new homes were to be constructed as part of the 'Homes fit for Heroes' post-war resettlement planning, but there is no evidence to suggest that even half this number of homes were ever actually built. Houses that were constructed were built to very high specifications for their time. At Killester, north of Dublin, one of the largest developments of 247 houses was built with nearly 800 ex-servicemen providing the labour. Fittingly, many of the names assigned to the new housing schemes recalled the war with names such as Messines Park in County Londonderry, Lille Park, also known as 'Soldier Town', located in Finaghy, South Belfast, and the extensive suburb positioned at Cregagh in East Belfast where nearly 150 homes were raised on six intersecting streets: Albert Drive, Bapaume Avenue, Picardy Avenue, Hamel Drive, Thiepval Avenue and Somme Drive. The majority of these houses are still occupied today.

Figure 6.9 Plan of Knowle Park, Bristol, c 1970, showing street layout with central square and cul-de-sacs, and essential amenities, as built in 1921 (Courtesy of Helen Caffrey)

Other, smaller developments were established such as Mons Terrace at Castlebar, County Mayo and Givenchy Terrace in Andersonstown, West Belfast, as well as many small clusters of 'soldiers' cottages' which even yet survive across Ireland.

Identification

These 'Homes fit for Heroes' were striking innovations, but appearances may have changed due to factors such as replacement windows, car ownership, refuse collection, and much private ownership since the 1980s. Council Minutes and local newspapers together with Ordnance Survey maps can help to pinpoint these estates, distinguishing them from rare early experiments (as at Wincobank in Sheffield) and later building under subsequent legislation. Houses built in experimental materials – various forms of concrete, metal frames such as Dorlonco, and early system building – have the lowest survival rate. In addition to the individual buildings, the location and layout of these estates with green spaces and no high-rise form a distinctive landscape. Visually and conceptually, this has been a lasting memorial in the aftermath of war.

Alternative approaches

Issues of food security and rural depopulation were already being addressed in the pre-war period, but the implications of the war in terms of employment for de-mobilised servicemen prompted further action. In 1916, and more fully in 1918, the Small Holding Colonies Acts enabled the Board of Agriculture and Fisheries to purchase land, and county councils as their agents to do the same, to facilitate small holding. In 1919 the Land Settlement (Facilities) Act gave more powers to county councils, enabling them for instance to borrow money and make loans to tenants to purchase livestock, seed and tools. The Act stated that 'preference should be given to suitable men' who had been in the forces and to 'suitable women certified by the Board' to have worked for a minimum of six months full-time in farming during the war; that priority was to run for two years, and the Act as a whole until 1926. One example is the purchase in 1920 by the West Riding County Council of land from the Wenlock Estate, to the south of York, which it then divided into small farms of about 32 acres (c 13ha) for returning servicemen. Each was provided with a small brick-built farmhouse. At Pembrey, Pembrokeshire, a Farm Colony was established through the Small Holdings Act 1920 which provided a colony of twelve houses built for the resettlement of soldiers and sailors. In Scotland, the Land Settlement Act of 1919 was used to create large numbers of small holdings for returning soldiers and the Scottish Board of Agriculture was empowered to assist with set-up costs.

Disability and unemployment

The King's National Roll Scheme (KNRS) was an innovative programme set up in 1919 to encourage firms to provide employment for the many thousands of disabled ex-servicemen. While the Scheme was not particularly successful in providing employment, partly on account of the difficulties of defining suitable work, and the anxieties of the trade unions, it did raise awareness of the issue. Firms that participated in the Scheme were entitled to use a special stamp on their letterhead and can be identified through documentary sources.

In Scotland, the village of Longniddry in East Lothian was gifted by the Earl of Wemyss to provide homes for wounded soldiers, as part of a very early Scottish Veterans' Garden City Association scheme. Construction started on the Arts and Crafts-style buildings in 1916 and the first veterans moved in in 1917. As well as a shop, village hall, beehives and a piggery in a local farm, a range of craft industries was set up. A total of 159 houses were built during and after the war, including some which were funded by donations from Caledonian societies and First Nation tribes in the USA.

An industrial village for partly disabled soldiers

Westfield, Lancaster, was the unique product of a partnership between Thomas Mawson (landscape architect and designer of several memorial public parks) and landowner Thomas Storey. The settlement was intended to provide on-site employment, recreation and companionship in surroundings of 'simple, direct, harmonious and pleasing restfulness'. Westfield looks back to Leverhulme's Port Sunlight and the dream of the English village with cottages around the bowling green. The community was small – a population of 49 men, 49 women and 155 children was recorded by 1930 – and its privacy defined by its distinctive gateway. Communal facilities included a clubhouse, provision for sports and (initially) workshops. Houses are named after battles and donors, and are built in a variety of styles on an axial layout. Its focus is the war memorial (Fig 6.10) symbolising compassion in its sculpture of an injured soldier being cared for by his companion.

However the houses show no specific physical provision for disability such as avoidance of steps.

The government rejected Mawson's plan for nationwide provision of such villages on the grounds that segregation was inappropriate. The houses are closer to Arts and Crafts in style than to Homes fit for Heroes, and were more expensive to build, set out with gardens and trees and to a plan closer to early Garden City ideals. This was a very personal and direct form of memorial to the war. Although not replicated, there may yet be similarly intentioned buildings awaiting identification.

Figure 6.10 The war memorial at the centre of the Westfield village for disabled soldiers in Lancaster (© Ivan Frontani)

CHAPTER 7

Afterword

Legacy and perceptions

Why is it that the impact of the First World War on the Home Front in Britain remains such a relatively unknown story, whose physical legacy has been so little explored? One factor is undoubtedly the point that within 20 years of the Peace being signed the country was yet again preparing for another world war, one which swept away or substantially modified many of the traces of the earlier conflict. But answers can perhaps also be found in the fact that for many, both at the time and later, the First World War was something that happened elsewhere, abroad. There was also a lack of clarity about what it had all been for, and whether fighting it had been worthwhile. The First World War's legacy is far more complex than is sometimes thought.

The war ended with the Armistice on 11 November 1918, although it was another seven months before the Peace Treaty was signed. The cost to the country had been enormous, although quite how much took a long time to quantify, and perhaps appreciate. The greatest cost, of course, was in lives, and even here it was unclear how many British servicemen had died. Until 30 years ago published estimates ranged between half a million and 1,200,000 and it was only in 1986 that the social historian Jay Winter assessed the true figure to be between 722,785 and 772,000: this remains generally accepted today. Far harder to quantify is the number who came home injured, whether physically or psychologically. For decades after the war men died prematurely from their injuries, or spent their lives in institutions, and in the late 1930s some 639,000 ex-servicemen were still drawing disability pensions. When men did come home to their families, a period of hard adjustment often followed, and for those who had lost husbands or fathers, the grief could be life-long.

The financial cost for Great Britain was around 35 billion dollars at 1913 values (in the order of £500 billion today). A government survey at the war's end helped define where the money had gone. Artillery production had risen from 91 guns a year in 1914 to 8039 in 1918, machine-guns from 300 to 121,000 and warplanes from 200 to 32,000. Over a million horses and mules had been purchased. Largely British manufactories produced an incredible range of war goods in often mind-boggling quantities: 136 million socks, 16 million ground sheets, and 46 million pairs of boots. Then there was the expenditure on Home Front infrastructure, as outlined in this *Handbook*, on camps, coastal defences, transport infrastructure, and building and converting factories and other plants.

But while hard figures such as these can be obtained, it is much more difficult to gauge what people's perceptions of the war were, both at the time and afterwards. Why is it that today – and in fact for many decades, if not from the time of the war itself – mention of the First *World* War to most people conjures up one of two images: of the mud of the Western Front, and of cemeteries and war memorials. The standard interpretative trajectory is that at the war's end the nation's grief and a need for remembrance found expression through the Cenotaph, the Tomb of the Unknown Warrior, and the tens of thousands of war memorials erected by communities across the land. Then came the 1920s, which were hard for many, followed at the end of that decade by a number of books – more fact than fiction – including Erich Maria Remarque's *All Quiet on the Western Front* (1929), Robert Graves' *Goodbye to All That* (1929), Siegfried Sassoon's *Memoirs of a Fox-Hunting Man* (1930) and *Memoirs of an Infantry* Officer (1930), along with R C Sheriff's play, *Journey's End* (1928; film version 1930). From the time they appeared these were perceived to have revealed for the first time the horror of the war: its true story.

But not all agree with this interpretation. In *The Great War: Myth and Memory* (2005) Dan Todman argued that experiences and perceptions of the war, certainly among the participants and their contemporaries, were more varied, and often positive. Graves was said to be surprised that his memoire was seen as anti-war: he claimed to have rather enjoyed aspects of his military service, while Sheriff's aim was not to write an anti-war play, but one which celebrated comradeship and duty. Similarly, while the economy was left indebted to the United States, and many were left injured or grieving, a significant number of the changes brought about by the war were positive ones. For instance, of necessity 'men of push and go' had seen to it that industrial production was transformed, with a new workforce employed on production lines in purpose-built factories with good welfare provision. Many of those workers were women, and their wages were spent on food, not drink: beer production halved over the war. Heavy transport shifted onto railways, and truck and car largely replaced the horse other than for very local traffic.

War surplus, trophies and thoughts of preservation

By the war's end there was massively more military infrastructure and materials than would be needed by a peacetime army. Moreover, rapid developments in technology meant that much was already redundant. Some sites and buildings returned to pre-war ownership and uses, or found a new role. Burton-on-Trent's machine-gun factory was bought by Crosse & Blackwell, and between 1922 and 1924 Branston Pickle was made there (see Fig 3.7). Many army huts were sold off and moved to become memorial halls, often the first time a community had had such a social facility. National Shipyard No 1 at Chepstow was disposed of in 1925: the shipyard was dismantled and the site used for the construction of large civil engineering projects such as bridges. Much heavy military hardware including vehicles and artillery came back from France via train-ferries to the new wartime port at Richborough (Kent), where already in late 1918, 800 mainly female workers

Figure 7.1 This tank
at Ashford in Kent
is the only surviving
example of the many
that were put on
display around the
country after the war
(© Wayne Cocroft)

were involved in processing salvage, principally shell cases. Where possible surplus materials were recycled or sold off rather than scrapped, with the Birmingham Small Arms Company handling war surplus rifles and machine-guns. Most of this work was handled out of sight on an industrial scale in factories and depots, often overseas. More visible were the German field guns presented by local regiments to their host communities, and the 265 'war battered' tanks awarded by the government to towns and cities which had excelled in fundraising during the war, which typically were displayed in parks and municipal gardens. But as so often, opinions were divided about such overt celebrations of warmongering; many guns and tanks were discretely got rid of over the next 20 years, with almost all the remainder going in the Second World War scrap drive. Only one tank survives, at Ashford (Kent), and is now a Grade II-listed structure (Fig 7.1).

One form of official remembrance was the Imperial War Museum, which was conceived in 1917 and opened in 1920. The intention was to collect and display material as a record of everyone's experiences during that war – civilian and military – and to commemorate the sacrifices of all sections of society. But as for sites and buildings which played a key part in the war there seems to have been little interest, unlike on the Western Front where key battlegrounds like Vimy Ridge (Fig 7.2) and Beaumont Hammel were identified for preservation virtually as soon as the fighting stopped, along with particular structures like the German bunkers around which the great Tyne Cot military cemetery developed. Just

Figure 7.2 While in Britain there was a focus on collecting artefacts associated with the war, on the Continent, key battlegrounds such as Vimy Ridge were quickly identified for preservation (Courtesy of Wayne Cocroft)

one example in Britain is known where it was recognised early on that military defences erected in 1914–18 might deserve protection. This was the consideration given in the late 1930s by the Ancient Monuments Board, working with the Office of Works (the predecessor to Historic England), to preserving certain pillboxes; but the Second World War intervened and nothing came of it.

Renewed interest in the First World War

Twenty years later the lead-up to the 50th anniversary of the outbreak of the First World War reawakened interest and led to new appraisals. In 1961, Alan Clark published *The Donkeys*, the origin of the popular view that the British army comprised 'lions led by donkeys', a view reinforced by the play and later film *Oh What a Lovely War*. That general perception, although not universally accepted, is now being challenged by the archaeological discovery of tens of sophisticated training trench systems where men were trained before embarking for the Western Front. As the wartime generation entered into retirement the ground-breaking BBC series *The Great War* (1964) introduced the war to a new and wider audience. The decade also saw a growing engagement with the war by social and economic historians.

In common with many other areas of archaeological study, interest in the traces of modern warfare has its origins with amateur collectors and enthusiasts. From the 1960s, growing leisure time, prosperity, and greater car ownership enabled devotees to visit abandoned fortifications and battlefields. In Britain, attention was initially focused on recovering mainly Second World War aircraft wrecks, although few if any excavations were carried out to professional archaeological standards. During the following decades various books appeared to serve this new interest, although some were little more than relic diggers' guides. Growing awareness in historic military buildings was also reflected in the formation of specialist societies, such as the Fortress Study Group in 1975 and two years later the Airfield Research Group. As described above, during the 1990s one of the most significant developments was the CBA-led Defence of Britain project, although fewer than 2% of the records created related directly to the First World War.

By the end of the decade archaeologists were applying professional excavation methods to the exploration of sections of the Western Front in France and Belgium, and further afield to the investigation of T E Lawrence's campaigns in Jordan. In the United Kingdom, excavations have investigated training trenches on the Otterburn ranges, Zeppelin crash sites, and a concrete training model on Cannock Chase.

The Home Front Legacy Project

This *Handbook* has been written to support the CBA's Home Front Legacy 1914–18 project which aims to encourage people to record the traces of the First World War in their area, be it through fieldwork, archives or oral history

Figure 7.3 The CBA's President Dan Snow recording First World War trenches at Gosport (Hants) with Stephen Fisher of CBA Wessex (© Wayne Cocroft)

(Fig 7.3). In common with the Defence of Britain project it looks to document former military sites such as army camps, drill halls, practice trenches and airfields, but it also seeks to record traces of the Home Front. Local research is critical to discover these places that were adapted for the war effort. The project will lead to a greater appreciation of the effects of First World War on the countryside, villages, towns and cities, and even on the sea bed. The supporting website is designed to allow individual researchers, or members of groups, to create professional standard electronic records for their local Historic Environment Records. An accompanying interactive map will chart the growing numbers of discoveries. These records will produce a permanent legacy of your research and of the effect of the war on the country. The identification and recognition of these sites is the first stage in their protection, securing these places, their memories and stories for future generations.

Sources

(Further details of books and articles can be found in the Bibliography)

Chapter 1

Key texts

N Bosanquet, *Our Land at War: Britain's key First World War sites* (2014)
B Lowry (ed), *20th century defences in Britain: An Introductory Guide* (1996)
N Saunders *et al*, 'The Home Front (1914–1918) and its Legacies: A pilot study for national public archaeology recording project of First World War legacies in Britain: 2014–2018' (https://www.historicengland.org.uk/images-books/publications/home-front-1914-1918-and-its-legacies/)
N J Saunders, *Killing time: Archaeology and the First World War* (revised edn 2010)

For a summary of the impact of the First World War in Wales, see A Gaffney's *Aftermath: remembering the Great War in Wales* (1998).

An appropriate starting point for a study of the First World War in Ireland is K Jeffery's *Ireland and the Great War*, while titles such as P Orr's, *The Road to the Somme*, R Grayson's *Belfast Boys* and T P Dooley's, *Irishmen or English Soldiers?* provide information on the social, economic, cultural and military impact of the First World War in Ireland, as well as analysis of important historical events leading to the formation of the Irish Divisions, their training, the journey to France, specific battles and the aftermath of war in Ireland and its effects on the different communities.

Websites

UK	Home Front Legacy: http://www.homefrontlegacy.org.uk.
	Pastmap: http://pastmap.org.uk/
	Britain from Above: http://www.britainfromabove.org.uk/
	The National Archives: http://www.nationalarchives.gov.uk/
	Imperial War Museum: http://www.iwm.org.uk/
England	*Pastscape*: http://www.pastscape.org.uk/
	Heritage Gateway: http://www.heritagegateway.org.uk/gateway/
	Historic England: http://www.historicengland.org.uk
Scotland	*Canmore*: http://canmore.rcahms.gov.uk/
	Historic Scotland: http://www.historic-scotland.gov.uk/

Historic Scotland and RCAHMS commissioned Dr Gordon Barclay to carry out an audit of the surviving built heritage of the First World War in Scotland. His report can be found at: http://www.rcahms.gov.uk/rcahms_media/files/publications/built_heritage_ww1_29nov2013.pdf

Wales	*Archwilio*: http://cofiadurcahcymru.org.uk/arch/
	Coflein: http://www.coflein.gov.uk/
	Cadw: http://cadw.wales.gov.uk/

JISC and the Welsh Government have funded a mass digitisation of primary sources relating to the First World War from the libraries, special collections and archives of Wales. This is available at: http://cymru1914.org/en

Reports on all of the Cadw-funded First World War projects will be available at: http://www.dyfedarchaeology.org.uk/ww1/index.html

Northern Ireland SMR: http://www.doeni.gov.uk/niea/built-home/built-home/recording/sites-and-monuments/ni-sites-and-monuments-record-database.htm

See also National Library of Ireland: http://www.nli.ie/

Recording field remains: terminology

Guidance on the correct terms to use when recording archaeological remains can be found at: http://fishforum.weebly.com/download-fish-terminology.html

In particular, see the First World War, Building Materials and Maritime thesauri.

Recording field remains: National Grid References (NGRs) can be accurately identified using: http://gridreferencefinder.com/gmap.php

Health and Safety Information

Specific advice on investigating archaeological sites can be found at the Home Front Legacy website: http://www.homefrontlegacy.org.uk/wp/site-safety/

More general Health and Safety guidance can be found at: http://www.hse.gov.uk/construction/safetytopics/index.htm

Chapter 2

Drill Halls

The two most useful sources for finding out more about drill halls are M Osborne's *Always ready; The Drill Halls of Britain's Volunteer Forces*, and http://www.drillhalls.org/ which contains a database of drill halls arranged by town within each country. This list is not exhaustive and some counties have, as yet, no entries. Kelly's Directories (widely available in Local Studies Libraries) include the addresses of drill halls and often a brief description of the facilities, whilst Ordnance Survey maps will clearly identify drill halls as named buildings. Katie Carmichael's national overview report on English drill halls is available online at: http://research.historicengland.org.uk/Report.aspx?i=15317&ru=%2fResults.aspx%3fp%3d1%26n%3d10%26a%3d4797%26ns%3d1.

For the history of the Territorial Army in its many guises see books such as *Britons, To Arms! The Story of the British Volunteer Soldier* by G A Stepple. Many local regiments will have dedicated and detailed literature, eg D Kelsall, *Stockport Lads Together, The 6th Cheshire Territorials, 1908–1919*.

Camps

There is an extensive range of literature on camps. James Douet's *British barracks 1600–1914: their architecture and role in society* provides an overview prior to the First World War. William Foot's 2006 study of Army Camps for English Heritage is also a useful starting point: http://archaeologydataservice.ac.uk/archives/view/armycamp_eh_2006. For an excellent synopsis of the raising of the New Armies from the political, social and economic perspective, including War Office Directives for the construction of camps and the specific training of the new recruits, see P Simkin's *Kitchener's Army, the Raising of the New Armies 1914–1916*. See also R Skinner, *Kitchener's Camp at Seaford, a First World War Landscape on Aerial Photograph; A town for four winters* by

C & G Whitehouse; and H Ullathorne's *Training Trenches at Redmires Sheffield, The Great War Remembered* which provides an authoritative report on the layout of Kitchener's camps and the elements expected therein. There are a number of books detailing the history of individual camps in Ireland; see for example P Orr's *Ballykinler Camp, The First Seven Decades, 1900–1969* and K Jordan's *Kilworth & Moore Park British Army Camps 1896–1922*.

A wide variety of places were used to house prisoners of war and internees and are listed in the books *Prisoners of War Information Bureau in London* and *List of Places of Internment*, reprinted by the Imperial War Museum. Yarnall discusses the experiences of prisoners in *Barbed wire disease: British & German Prisoners of War, 1914–19*. Recent publications on individual camps include Chapman and Moss' *Detained in England 1914–1920: Eastcote POW Camp, Pattishall* and details of the recent survey at Felday Camp by Surrey Archaeological Society (http://www.surreyarchaeology.org.uk/) can be found in: Newell & Winser, 'Felday World War 1 Prisoner of War camp: an archaeological survey' (typescript report by Surrey Archaeological Society 2013).

Internment

W J Brennan-Whitmore, *With the Irish in Frongoch* provides an eye-witness account of the events and regimes experienced by Irish Volunteers within Frongoch during their period of internment.

For a guide to internment on the Isle of Man in both the First and Second World Wars see: http://www.manxnationalheritage.im/wp-content/uploads/2013/08/CG4-Internment_Web.pdf

Practice trenches

There are numerous books and articles about trench warfare. Key texts include Martin Brown's 'Reflections of War' (2008); Brown and Osgood's *Digging up Plugstreet* (2008); P Doyle's *Tommy's War* (2008) and Brown and Field's 'Training trenches on Salisbury Plain: archaeological evidence for battle training in the Great War'.

Contemporary sources include Graham Seton Hutchinson's *Machine guns: their history and tactical employment (being also a history of the machine gun corps, 1916–1922)*, published in 1938, and various War Office documents such as *Manual of Fieldworks (All Arms)* (1921). Recent studies on local defensive works include Victor Smith's article on the north Kent coast (2014) and Peter Chasseaud's work on Sussex (2014).

Hospitals

Detailed histories of individual hospitals include Alper's 1997 volume on Roehampton and Hoare's *Spike Island: The Memory of a Military Hospital*. For a general overview see Brian Abel-Smith, *The Hospitals, 1800–1948*.

The *London Gazette* (https://www.thegazette.co.uk/) listed all decorations awarded, including those given to hospital staff.

The Suburban Birmingham website (http://www.suburbanbirmingham.org.uk/) has interesting images of the Southern General hospital which was housed in the Aston Webb building at the University of Birmingham.

Many stately homes and public buildings are holding exhibitions about their role in the First World War. For local exhibitions and events see websites such as:
Historic England http://www.historicengland.org.uk
National Trust http://www.nationaltrust.org.uk/
Brighton Pavilion http://www.brighton-hove-rpml.org.uk/RoyalPavilion/Pages/home.aspx

Chapter 3

Easter Rising

For an excellent digital account visit www.easter1916.ie

See also Louise Jefferson's *Dublin then and now: scenes from a revolutionary city* and *The Easter Rising: A Guide to Dublin 1916* by Kostick & Collins

Industry

Factories of all kinds were involved in war work; the best sources for indentifying the work undertaken are local newspapers and company records. These can generally be found in Local Studies Libraries. A good introduction to industrial manufacturing processes is the CBA's *Industrial Archaeology: A Handbook* by Palmer *et al* (2012).

Information on specialist industries, such as explosives, can be found in Cocroft's *Dangerous Energy The archaeology of gunpowder and military explosives manufacture* (2000) or Edmonds' 2004 volume *The History of Rotherwas Munitions Factory, Hereford*. *The History of the Ministry of Munitions*, published by HMSO in 12 volumes in 1920–22, is now available as a Naval and Military Press reprint. Kenyon's report for Historic England 'First World War National Factories An archaeological, architectural, and historical review' provides information on the survival of factories in England. For Ireland, see Kelleher 1993, *Gunpowder to guided missiles: Ireland's war industries*.

Mark Swenarton's *Homes fit for Heroes* (1981) gives an account of wartime and post-war state housing and the munitions workers' estate at Mancot was written up in the *Architects' and Builders' Journal* in December 1918 (vol **48**). It also features in T W Pritchard's *A History of the Old Parish of Hawarden* (2002).

Transport

For a comprehensive description of the railway network and wartime activities see: E A Pratt (1921) *British Railways and the Great War*, which is available at Cornell University Library: https://archive.org/details/cu31924092566136.

A more digestible overview can be found in *Britain's railways at war 1914–18* (Earnshaw 1990), while Vallance (1938) describes the impact of the war on the Highland Line in *A History of the Highland Railway*.

The canal network was nationalised in 1948 and, after various reorganisations, was run by the British Waterways Board. This was wound up in 2012 and responsibility for leisure use of canals passed to the Canals and Rivers Trust, which also assumed responsibility for canal historic records. These records are now held by the National Waterways Museum in Ellesmere Port. There is an extensive online catalogue. Useful links are: https://canalrivertrust.org.uk/national-waterways-museum/the-museum-collections/the-waterways-archive and http://www.virtualwaterways.co.uk/Home.html.

In addition, many of the individual canal trusts, such as the Basingstoke Canal Society (http://www.basingstoke-canal.org.uk/), hold their own archives.

Agriculture

There is much in print on agriculture in the First World War; the most specific study is P E Dewey, *British Agriculture in the First World War*. Other short studies which can be recommended are Jonathan Brown, *Agriculture in England: A Survey of Farming, 1870–1947* and Richard Perren, *Agriculture in Depression, 1870–1940*. For mechanisation, Jonathan Brown's *Farm Machinery 1750–1945* is well-illustrated, and strong on agricultural context.

Wartime forestry is briefly covered in N D G James, *A History of English Forestry*, while the Shire book *Allotments* by Twigs Way is engaging and fact-packed.

Conscientious Objectors

Data from the *Pearce Register of British Conscientious Objectors* have been added to the IWM's *Lives of the First World War* website: http://livesofthefirstworldwar.org/. There it is possible to search for individual, named Conscientious Objectors or to explore the full range of the data in tabular or datasheet form.

Hardly anything has been published dealing specifically with the detail of Conscientious Objector work schemes. The standard texts on the subject list them but are tantalisingly short on detail. These include: J W Graham, *Conscription and Conscience – a history 1916–1919* (1922); David Boulton, *Objection Overruled* (1967); John Rae, *Conscience and Politics: The British Government and the Conscientious Objector to Military Service 1916–1919* (1970). Reports from the Brace Committee to the House of Commons are useful sources and can be found in Hansard. Reports in the local press may be more rewarding.

Chapter 4

A good starting point for the history of fortifications is Andrew Saunders' *Fortress Britain* (1989). Colin Dobinson's typescript report 'Coast Artillery, 1900–56' (1999) deals specifically with the 20th century and includes a gazetteer of sites.

For Wales, see J D Davies' *Britannia's Dragon: a Naval history of Wales* (2013).

Wireless

A good starting point for early wireless in Britain, in particular the work of Marconi and the development of the Marconi Company, is *A History of the Marconi Company* by W J Baker. In providing an overview spanning more than fifty years it is, however, a little sparse on the development of wireless and signals intelligence.

Three excellent publications which include material on signals intelligence during the First World War are Patrick Beesly's *Room 40: British Naval Intelligence 1914–1918*; Peter Matthews' *SIGINT: The Secret History of Signals Intelligence 1914–45*; and *GCHQ: The Secret Wireless War, 1900–86* by Nigel West. Two further publications on the development of signalling, in particular wireless, in the navy are: *The Electron and Sea Power* (Hezlet 1975) and *Signal! A History of Signalling in the Royal Navy* (Kent 1993). Oxford Archaeology has produced a typescript report for Historic England (forthcoming) on 'First World War Wireless Stations in England'. This lists all the pre-1919 stations in England, some of whose precise locations remain unknown.

Signals intelligence and wireless signalling during the First World War was not the sole preserve of the Royal Navy and the definitive source on the Royal Engineers Signal Service during the First World War is R E Priestley's *The Signal Service in the European War of 1914 to 1918 (France)*. Last and definitely not least, the following publication provides excellent technical details of the wireless sets used during the First World War and beyond: Louis Meulstee, *Wireless for the Warrior. Compendium 1: Spark to Larkspur (Wireless Sets 1910–1948)*.

Dockyards

Key texts which provide a broad overview include:
J Coad, *Support for the Fleet* (2013)
D Evans, *Arming the Fleet: The development of the Royal Ordnance Yards 1770–1945* (2006)
P Brown, *Britain's Historic Ships* (2009)

For information on specific yards, see:

P Brown, *Maritime Portsmouth* (2009)

B Patterson, *Give'er a Cheer Boys: The Great Docks of Portsmouth Dockyard* (1989)

R Riley, The Evolution of the Docks and Industrial Buildings in Portsmouth Royal Dockyard,
   Portsmouth Papers, No 44 (1985)

Portsmouth Historic Dockyard: http://www.historicdockyard.co.uk/

P MacDougall, *Chatham Dockyard: The Rise and Fall of a Military Industrial Complex* (2012)

Chatham Historic Dockyard: http://www.thedockyard.co.uk/

Chatham Maritime Trust: http://www.cmtrust.co.uk/content/about/history.rhtm

Devonport (Plymouth) Dockyard: http://www.plymouth.gov.uk/hm_naval_base_devonport_free_
   tours.pdf; http://www.plymouthnavalmuseum.com

Scapa Flow

There is an extensive body of literature on Scapa Flow. The following items are recommended:

Geoffrey Stell, *Orkney at War: Defending Scapa Flow, volume 1, World War I* (2011), which contains
   a full bibliography;

W S Hewison, *This Great Harbour Scapa Flow* (1985; new edn 2005)

Angus Konstam, *Scapa Flow: The defences of Britain's fleet anchorage 1914–45* (2009)

Ships and shipwrecks

Contemporary sources include:

Board of Trade, *Return of Shipping Casualties and Loss of Life for the Period Ended 31st December
   1918* (1921)

T Dorling, *Swept Channels, being an account of the work of the minesweepers in the Great War* (1935)

E Keble Chatterton, *Q-ships and their story* (1922)

S Sassoon, *Memoirs of an Infantry Officer* (1930)

More modern accounts include:

F J Dittmar & J J Colledge, *British Warships 1914–1919* (1972)

I Friel, *Maritime History of Britain and Ireland* (2003)

W Mitchell & L A Sawyer, *British Standard Ships of World War I* (1968)

Ian Wilson, *HMS Drake: Rathlin Island shipwreck* (Rathlin 2011) provides a comprehensive
   narrative into the life and indeed the demise of HMS Drake.

For information on all aspects of historic ships, see: http://www.nationalhistoricships.org.uk/
index.php

The Historic England website contains a number of reports:

Military Aircraft Crash Sites (2002)

https://www.historicengland.org.uk/images-books/publications/military-aircraft-crash-sites/

Ships and Boats: 1840 to 1950 (2012)

https://www.historicengland.org.uk/images-books/publications/iha-ships-boats-1840-1950/

Designation Selection Guide Ships and Boats: Prehistory to Present

https://www.historicengland.org.uk/listing/selection-criteria/wreck-selection/

M Dunkley (2013) 'Defending the East Coast – investigating England's forgotten war channels',
   Conservation Bulletin **71**. https://www.historicengland.org.uk/images-books/publications/
   conservation-bulletin-71/

A Firth (2014) 'East Coast War Channels in the First and Second World Wars'; typescript report
   for Historic England. https://www.historicengland.org.uk/images-books/publications/east-
   coast-war-channels-first-and-second-world-wars/

The UNESCO *Code of Ethics for Diving on Underwater Cultural Heritage Sites* can be found at:
http://www.unesco.org/new/en/culture/themes/underwater-cultural-heritage/divers/code-of-ethics/

Chapter 5

Airfields and airship stations

Information on records relating to the Royal Air Force and related material held by The National Archives can be found at: http://www.nationalarchives.gov.uk/records/research-guides/raf-op.htm (see also: TNA AIR 1 452/15/312/26).

The Airfield Information Exchange contains the archive and forum for the Airfield Research Group. The archive aims to conserve, as far as possible, documentation in all media formats pertaining to the airfields and associated locations in the United Kingdom and, where necessary, overseas.
http://www.airfieldinformationexchange.org/

The Airfields of Britain Conservation Trust has been compiling an inventory of airfields including disused ones.
http://www.abct.org.uk/airfields/orfordness

Information on specific historic airfields can be found on individual websites:
Calshot: www.hants.gov.uk/calshot
Cosford: www.rafmuseum.org.uk
Duxford: www.iwm.org.uk/visits/iwm-duxford
East Fortune: http://www.nms.ac.uk/national-museum-of-flight/
Farnborough: www.airsciences.org.uk
Hendon: www.rafmuseum.org.uk
Hooton Park: www.hootonparktrust.co.uk
Montrose: www.rafmontrose.org.uk
Old Sarum: www.oldsarum.co.uk
Stow Maries: www.stowmaries.com

Useful further reading on airfields and airship stations includes:
Action Stations: A series with various authors and dates, it provides short histories of most UK airfields
P Francis, *British military airfield architecture from airships to the jet age* (1996)
J Lake, 'Historic airfields: evaluation and conservation', in Schofield *et al* (2002)
T Biblé, *Kingsnorth Airship Station In defence of the nation* (2013)
D Brock, *Wings over Carew* (1989)
C Mowthorpe, *Battlebags: British airships of the First World War* (1998)
G D Hay & G P Stell, *Monuments of Industry an illustrated historical record* (1986)

See also: English Heritage (2003) *Historic Military Aviation Sites – conservation management guidance.*
http://www.historicengland.org.uk/images-books/publications/historic-military-aviation-sites/

Air raids and anti-aircraft sites

C Dobinson, 'Acoustics and radar England's early warning systems 1915–45' (2000) includes a gazetteer of sites.
C Dobinson, *AA Command: Britain's Anti-aircraft defences of the Second World War* (2001)
I Castle, *London 1914–17: The Zeppelin menace* (2008)
I Castle, *London 1917–18: The Bomber blitz* (2010)
N Faulkner & N Durrani, *In search of the Zeppelin War The archaeology of the First Blitz* (2008)
F Pile, *Ack-Ack Britain's defence against air attack during the Second World War* (1949)
E Dwyer, *The impact of the railways in the East End 1835–2010: historical archaeology from the London Overground East London Line* (2011)
C Dobinson, *Building radar: forging Britain's early warning chain 1935–45* (2010) contains useful background information on First World War sites.

Chapter 6

A starting point for the study of war commemoration in Britain is A King's *Memorials of the Great War in Britain: the symbolism and politics of remembrance*. Another excellent book is J Winter, *Sites of Memory, Sites of Mourning: the Great War in European Cultural History*. For a study covering the concept of the war memorial in its historical context, see A Borg, *War Memorials: from antiquity to the present*.

A good survey of the impact of medieval imagery on war memorials is S Goebel's *The Great War and Medieval Memory: war, remembrance and medievalism in Britain and Germany 1914–1940*.

There are several excellent regional reviews of the commemorative process; see as examples M Connelly, *The Great War, Memory and Ritual: commemoration in the City and East London, 1916–1939* and N C Johnson's *Ireland, the Great War and the Geography of Remembrance*.

War memorials

War Memorials Trust works to protect and conserve war memorials in the UK; it manages the War Memorials Online project asking the public to add or update the condition of their local war memorials. See: www.warmemorialsonline.org.uk

Some examples of different types of memorial can be seen at:
Llandaff cathedral: www.warmemorialsonline.org.uk/node/164598
St Peter and St Paul, Bardwell: www.warmemorialsonline.org.uk/node/132200
Preston: www.warmemorialsonline.org.uk/node/134470
Datchet: http://datchethistory.org.uk/articles/village-greens/how-many-war-memorials/

Information on cemeteries in the care of the Commonwealth War Graves Commission can be found at: www.cwgc.org.uk

Village halls

ACRE (Action with Communities in Rural England) supports the 38 existing Rural Community Councils by facilitating the national Village Hall Information Service. ACRE has published a wide-ranging series of over 40 leaflets on Village Halls. These include detailed guidance on dealing with issues from Planning Fees and the Role of Trustees, through to Village Hall Maintenance, Heating and Flooring. A full list of current publications can be found on their website: http://www.acre.org.uk/our-work/community-assets/village-hall-information-service

Parks and gardens

Parks & Gardens UK is currently developing a national gazetteer and inviting submissions via http://www.parksandgardens.org/

Historic England has published an overview of war memorial parks and gardens, available at: https://www.historicengland.org.uk/images-books/publications/iha-war-memorial-parks-gardens/

Homes fit for Heroes

The most useful source is the Local Government Board's *Manual for State-Aided Housing Schemes*, produced in 1919 to help local authorities implement the Act. More may be found in the 1918 *Tudor Walters Report*, and the influential *Interim Report of the Women's Housing Sub-Committee*, 1917. Contemporary issues of the *Town Planning Review* and *The Builder* offer an informed commentary. The housing context is covered in Stephen Merrett's *State Housing in Britain* (1979), in Stuart Lowe and David Hughes (eds), *A New Century of Social Housing* (1991), and Richard Rodger's (ed) *Scottish Housing in the Twentieth Century* (1989). Detailed case studies appear in M J Daunton's

Councillors and Tenants: Local Authority Housing in England 1919–39 (1984), while information on individual London boroughs may be found in the *Survey of London* (http://www.british-history. ac.uk/search/series/survey-london). Mervyn Miller's biography, *Raymond Unwin: Garden Cities and Town Planning* (1992), also discusses *Homes fit for Heroes* and the evolution of the underlying ideas. An overview of the scheme can be found in M Swenarton's *Homes fit for Heroes: The politics and architecture of early state housing in Britain* (1981).

Meaghan Kowalsky's article 'This Honourable Obligation: the KNRS for Disabled Ex-servicemen 1915–44' in *European Review of History* (2007) discusses the impact of the KNRS in general, while Carol Lockwood's article 'From Soldier to Peasant? The Land Settlement Scheme in East Sussex, 1919–1939' (*Albion* 30, 1998) provides a local perspective.

Mawson's vision for Westfield may be seen through his booklet *An Imperial Obligation* (1917), and in his 1919 brochure *The War Memorial Village, Westfield, Lancaster* (available on the King's Own Royal Regiment website: http://www.kingsownmuseum.plus.com/westfield001.htm). Sharon Vernon's article in the *Lancashire Local Historian* 16 (2003), explains the issues.

For details of the scheme in Ireland, see:

Homes for Irish Heroes – Housing under the Irish Land (Provision for Soldiers & Sailors) Act 1919, and F H A Aalen's article 'Irish Sailors' & Soldiers' Land Trust' in *Town Planning Review* 59.

Chapter 7

The best recent discussion of the changing perceptions of the First World War is David Reynold's *The Long Shadow* (2013); the issues were also discussed by Dan Todman in *The Great War: Myth and Memory* (2005). The staggering material cost of the war was officially documented in *Statistics of the Military Effort of the British Empire during the Great War* (HMSO 1922) and the cultural history of memory and mourning is discussed by Jay Winter (1995).

Details on the Home Front Legacy project may be found on its dedicated website http://www. homefrontlegacy.org.uk.

Figure references

Details of images sourced from national and local archives are given below, with reference numbers where known. Images not listed have come either from private collections or are available online.

Fig	Subject	© holder	Reference (where known)
1.1	Excavation of a mass grave at Pheasant Wood, Fromelles	Oxford Archaeology	
1.3	Women workers at the National Shell Factory, Parkgate, Dublin	IWM	Q33212
1.5	Workers' huts at the National Factory, Gretna	RCAHMS/Aerofilms Archive	SPW027440
1.6	The large military training camp at Stobs, OS map 1920	National Library of Scotland	Roxburghshire Sheet n024.13, 1920
1.7	National Projectile Munitions Factory, Hall Street, Dudley	English Heritage	BB88/07422
2.1	First World War trenches at Barry Buddon Training Centre	RCAHMS	DP 176273
2.3	Golspie Volunteer Drill Hall	RCAHMS	SC 684599
2.4	Queen's Own Cameron Highlanders Barracks, Inverness	RCAHMS	SC 1315496
2.8	56 Davies Street, HQ for Queen Victoria and St George's Rifles	English Heritage	BL13472
2.9	Bell tents at Kilworth Camp, Co Cork	National Library of Ireland	EAS_0897e 17934
2.14	Contemporary photograph of Stobs Camp, near Hawick	RCAHMS	DP 198936
2.16	First World War training trenches, Browndown, Hants	English Heritage/RAF Collection	RAF540 453 fr 4185, 1951
2.20	Distribution of First World War trench systems on Forth and Tay estuaries	RCAHMS	
2.22	Invergordon Naval Hospital under construction	RCAHMS	DP 196205
2.23	Aston Webb building, University of Birmingham	University of Birmingham	BU-ATW-098
2.24	An amputee recovering at Roehampton Hospital	English Heritage	BL24278
2.25	Aerial view of Netley Hospital, Hants taken in 1923	English Heritage	EPW009063
2.26	UVF hospital wing, Queen's University Belfast, 1915	Somme Museum	
3.1	Damage caused to the barracks at Scarborough Castle during bombardment, 16 December 1914	English Heritage	FL01032_02_009
3.3	Aerial view of the National Projectile Factory, Hackney	English Heritage	EPW005749
3.4	Coupled shed at RAF Leuchars with Belfast truss roof	RCAHMS	DP 006325
3.8	North Eastern Railway Shell Shop, Darlington	Pratt 1921	facing p 596
3.10	Wreckage of National Shell Filling Factory, Chilwell, after explosion on 1 July 1918	English Heritage	AA96_03583
3.11	The Gretna Township	English Heritage	JLP01/01/113/18

Fig	Subject	© holder	Reference (where known)
3.13a	The train ferry loading bridge at Richborough	Sandwich Guildhall Archive	
3.14	The only known photograph of an Admiralty coal train	John Alsop Collection	
3.15	German PoWs unloading timber at Frimley Wharf	Basingstoke Canal Society	
3.19	Plan of the Swaythling Remount Depot	The National Archives	WO161/117
3.23	Painting of the camp at Caolas-na-con, Kinlochleven	RCAHMS	SC 1403508
4.2	Bull Sand Fort, off Spurn Point, River Humber	English Heritage	20620/045
4.4	Hoxa Head 4-inch coast battery, S Ronaldsay	RCAHMS	SC_06_600937
4.6	Plan of battery at Spurn Point	The National Archives	WO78-4312
4.7	Cross-section of a blockhouse, Forth Bridge defences	The National Archives	WO78-4396
4.10	Plan & cross-section of 6" gun emplacement, Lavernock	The National Archives	WO78-2281
4.16	Aerial view of the lighthouse and radio intercept station, Hunstanton, Norfolk	English Heritage	EPW001849
4.20	The 250-ton cantilever crane at Rosyth	RCAHMS	SC 349169
4.21	Portsmouth Dockyard, 1904	Portsmouth Museums & Record Service	Peskett-Frost Collection
4.22	Coast Battery at Roan Head, Flotta	RCAHMS	SC 1166329
4.27	Sonar image of the SMS *Markgraf*, Scapa Flow	ScapaMap	
4.29	Remains of U Boat in Medway Estuary, Kent	English Heritage	NMR27196_027
5.1	Isometric drawing of the side door hangar at Montrose	RCAHMS	SC 367620
5.6	Stannergate seaplane hangar	RCAHMS	SC 361983
5.7	Inchinnan airship shed under construction , 1916	RCAHMS	SC 684437
5.8	Aerial view of airship sheds, Cardington, Bedfordshire	English Heritage	27516/02
5.9b	RNAS Pembroke (Milton) Air Station	NMRW	AP_2013_5185
5.10	Reconstruction painting of Lodge Hill Anti-aircraft Battery	English Heritage	
5.11	Recently uncovered acoustic mirrors at Fan Bay, Dover	National Trust	
5.13	Air-raid shelters at Royal Gunpowder Factory, Waltham Abbey, Essex	Royal Gun Powder Mills	
6.8	Experimental 'Waller' pannelled concrete houses, Crossgates Estate, Leeds	Leeds Library & Information Service	Leodis 765

Bibliography

Aalen, F H A, 1988 Homes for Irish Heroes – Housing under the Irish Land (Provision for Soldiers & Sailors) Act 1919, and the Irish Sailors' & Soldiers' Land Trust, *Town Planning Review* **59**(3), 305–23

Ainsworth, S, 1990 A light railway on Stanton Moor, Derbyshire, *Industrial Railway Record* **122**, 149–53

Allen, J R L, 2000 National Shipyard No.2, Beachley, Gloucestershire: some ceramic evidence from the First World War, *Post-Medieval Archaeology* **34**, 203–06

Alper, H (ed), 1997 *A History of Queen Mary's University Hospital, Roehampton*. Roehampton: The Trust

Baker, W J, 1970 *A History of the Marconi Company*. London: Methuen

Barclay, G, 2013 *The built heritage of the First World War in Scotland*. Available at: http://www.rcahms.gov.uk/rcahms_media/files/publications/built_heritage_ww1_29nov2013.pdf. Accessed 3 March 2015

Beesly, P, 1984 *Room 40: British Naval Intelligence 1914–1918*. Oxford: Oxford University Press

Biblé, T, 2013 *Kingsnorth Airship Station In defence of the nation*. Stroud: The History Press

Board of Trade, 1921 *Return of Shipping Casualties and Loss of Life for the Period Ended 31st December 1918*. London: HMSO

Borg, A, 1991 *War Memorials: from antiquity to the present*. London: Leo Cooper

Bosanquet, N, 2014 *Our Land at War: Britain's key First World War sites*. Stroud: The History Press

Boulton, D, 1967 *Objection Overruled*. London: Macgibbon and Kee

Brennan-Whitmore, W J, 2013 *With the Irish in Frongoch*. Cork: Mercier Press

Brock, D, 1989 *Wings over Carew*. Pembroke: Deric Brock

Brown, G and Field, D, 2007 Training trenches on Salisbury Plain: archaeological evidence for battle training in the Great War, *Wiltshire Archaeological & Natural History Magazine* **100**, 170–80

Brown, J, 1987 *Agriculture in England: A Survey of Farming, 1870–1947*. Manchester: Manchester University Press

Brown, J, 1989 *Farm Machinery 1750–1945*. London: Batsford

Brown, M & Osgood, R, 2009 *Digging up Plugstreet*. Sparkford: Haynes

Brown, P, 2009 *Maritime Portsmouth*. Stroud: The History Press

Brown, P, 2009 *Britain's Historic Ships*. London: Conway

Castle, I, 2008 *London 1914–17: The Zeppelin menace*. Oxford: Osprey

Castle, I, 2010 *London 1917–18: The Bomber blitz*. Oxford: Osprey

Chapman, C R & Moss, S R, 2012 *Detained in England 1914–1920: Eastcote POW Camp, Pattishall*. Dursley: Lochin Publishing

Chasseaud, P, 2014 A mirror to Armageddon The landscape of Sussex in the First World War: trench systems, defence plans and military training in Sussex 1914–1918, *Sussex Archaeological Collections* **152**, 153–87

Coad, J, 2013 *Support for the Fleet*. London: English Heritage

Cocroft, W D, 2000 *Dangerous Energy The archaeology of gunpowder and military explosives manufacture*. Swindon: English Heritage

Cocroft, W D and Leith, I, 1996 Cunard's Shellworks, Liverpool, *Archive* **11**, 53–64

Connelly, M, 2001 *The Great War, Memory and Ritual: commemoration in the City and East London, 1916–1939*. London: Royal Historical Society

Daunton, M J (ed), 1984 *Councillors and Tenants: Local Authority Housing in English cities 1919–39*. Leicester: Leicester University Press

Davies, J D, 2013 *Britannia's Dragon: a Naval history of Wales*. Stroud: The History Press

Dewey, P E , 1989 *British Agriculture in the First World War*. Routledge

Dittmar, F J & Colledge, J J, 1972 *British Warships 1914–1919*. London: Allan

Dobinson, C, 1999 Coast Artillery 1900–56. Twentieth Century Fortifications in England Volume VI (typescript report). York: Council for British Archaeology

Dobinson, C, 2000 Acoustics and radar England's early warning systems 1915–45. Twentieth Century Fortifications in England Volume VII (typescript report). York: Council for British Archaeology

Dobinson, C, 2001 *AA Command: Britain's Anti-aircraft defences of the Second World War*. London: Methuen

Dobinson, C, 2010 *Building radar: forging Britain's early warning chain 1935–45*. London: Methuen

Dooley, T P, 1995 *Irishmen or English Soldiers?* Liverpool: Liverpool University Press

Dorling, T, 1935 *Swept Channels being an account of the work of the minesweepers in the Great War*. London: Hodder & Stoughton

Douet, J, 1998 *British barracks 1600–1914 : their architecture and role in society*. London: HMSO

Doyle, P, 2008 *Tommy's War*. Marlborough: Crowood

Dunkley, M, 2013 Defending the East Coast – investigating England's forgotten war channels, *Conservation Bulletin* **71** (Winter 2013), 26–7. Available at: https://www.historicengland.org.uk/images-books/publications/conservation-bulletin-71/. Accessed 7 April 2015

Dwyer, E, 2011 *The impact of the railways in the East End 1835–2010: historical archaeology from the London Overground East London Line*, MOLA Monograph **52**. London: Museum of London

Edmonds, J, 2004 *The History of Rotherwas Munitions Factory, Hereford*. Logaston: Logaston Press

Edwards, B, 1994 National Filling Factory No.5 Quedgley, *J Gloucestershire Soc Industrial Archaeol*, 32–52

Evans, D, 2006 *Arming the Fleet The development of the Royal Ordnance Yards 1770–1945*. Gosport: Explosion! Museum and English Heritage

Faulkner, N and Durrani, N, 2008 *In search of the Zeppelin War The archaeology of the First Blitz*. Stroud: Tempus

Firth, A, 2014 East Coast War Channels in the First and Second World War; typescript report for English Heritage. Available at: https://www.historicengland.org.uk/images-books/publications/east-coast-war-channels-first-and-second-world-wars/. Accessed 7 April 2015

Francis, P, 1996 *British military airfield architecture from airships to the jet age*. Sparkford: Patrick Stephens Ltd

Friel, I, 2003 *Maritime History of Britain and Ireland*. London: The British Museum Press

Gaffney, A, 1998 *Aftermath: remembering the Great War in Wales*. Cardiff: University of Wales Press

Goebel, S, 2007 *The Great War and Medieval Memory: war, remembrance and medievalism in Britain and Germany 1914–1940*. Cambridge: Cambridge University Press

Graham, J W, 1922 *Conscription and Conscience – a history 1916–1919*. London: G Allen & Unwin

Grayson, R, 2009 *Belfast Boys: how Unionists and Nationalists fought and died together in the First World War*. London: Continuum

Hay, G D and Stell, G P, 1986 *Monuments of Industry an illustrated historical record*. Edinburgh: RCAHMS

Hewison, W S, 2005 *This Great Harbour Scapa Flow*. 1st edn Kirkwall, 1985; new edn Edinburgh, 2005

Hezlet, A, 1975 *The Electron and Sea Power*. London: P Davies

HMSO, 1920–22 *The History of the Ministry of Munitions*. (12 vols) [Available as a Naval and Military Press reprint]

HMSO, 1922 *Statistics of the Military Effort of the British Empire during the Great War 1914–20*. [Available as a Naval and Military Press reprint 1999]

James, N D G, 1981 *A History of English Forestry*. Oxford: Blackwell

Jefferson, L, 2006 *Dublin then and now: scenes from a revolutionary city*. Belfast: Brehon Press

Jeffery, K, 2000 *Ireland and the Great War*. New York: Cambridge University Press

Johnson, N C, 2003 *Ireland, the Great War and the Geography of Remembrance.* Cambridge: Cambridge University Press

Jordan, K, 2004 *Kilworth & Moore Park British Army Camps 1896–1922.* Cork: Strawhall Press

Keble Chatterton, E, 1922 *Q-ships and their story.* London: Sidgwick & Jackson

Kelleher, G D, 1993 *Gunpowder to guided missiles Ireland's war industries.* Ireland: Privately printed

Kelsall, D, 1989 *Stockport Lads Together, The 6th Cheshire Territorials, 1908–1919,* Stockport: Stockport Metropolitan Borough Council

Kent, B, 1993 *Signal! A History of Signalling in the Royal Navy.* Clanfield: Hyden House

Kenyon, D, forthcoming 'First World War National Factories An archaeological, architectural, and historical review'. Historic England research report

King, A, 1998 *Memorials of the Great War in Britain: the symbolism and politics of remembrance.* Oxford: Berg

Konstam, A, 2009 *Scapa Flow: The defences of Britain's fleet anchorage 1914–45.* Oxford: Botley

Kostick, C & Collins, L, 2000 *The Easter Rising: A Guide to Dublin 1916.* Dublin: O'Brien Press

Kowalsky, M, 2007, This Honourable Obligation: the KNRS for Disabled Ex-servicemen 1915–44, *European Review of History* **14**(4), 567–84

Lake, J, 2002 Historic airfields: evaluation and conservation, in J Schofield, W G Johnson and C M Beck (eds), *Matériel Culture: the archaeology of twentieth century conflict.* Routledge: One World Archaeology **44**, 172–88

Lewis, J, 1999 *London's Lea Valley Britain's best kept secret.* Chichester: Phillimore

Lockwood, C, 1998 From Soldier to Peasant? The Land Settlement Scheme in East Sussex, 1919–1939, *Albion* **30**, 439–62

Lowe, S and Hughes, D (eds), 1991 *A New Century of Social Housing.* Leicester: Leicester University Press

Lowry, B (ed), 1996 *20th century defences in Britain: An Introductory Guide,* CBA Practical Handbook **12.** York: Council for British Archaeology

Lucas, E, 1935 *Light Buildings.* London: The Technical Press

MacDougall, P, 2012 *Chatham Dockyard: The Rise and Fall of a Military Industrial Complex.* Stroud: The History Press

Matthews, P, 2013 *SIGINT: The Secret History of Signals Intelligence 1914–45.* Stroud: The History Press

Merrett, S, 1979 *State Housing in Britain.* London: Routledge & Keegan Paul

Meulstee, L, 2009 *Wireless for the Warrior. Compendium 1: Spark to Larkspur (Wireless Sets 1910–1948).* Groenlo: Emaus Uitgeverij

Miller, M, 1992 *Raymond Unwin: Garden Cities and Town Planning.* Leicester: Leicester University Press

Mitchell, W and Sawyer, L A, 1968 *British Standard Ships of World War I.* Liverpool: Sea Breezes

Mowthorpe, C, 1998 *Battlebags: British airships of the First World War.* Stroud: Wrens Park

O'Brien, T, 1991 *The Things They Carried.* London: Flamingo

Orr, P, 2008 *The Road to the Somme.* Belfast: Blackstaff Press

Orr, P, 2012 *Ballykinler Camp, The First Seven Decades, 1900–1969.* Down County Museum

Osborne, M, 2006 *Always ready; The Drill Halls of Britain's Volunteer Forces.* Leigh-on-Sea: Partizan Press

Oxford Archaeology, forthcoming 'First World War Wireless Stations in England'; typescript report for Historic England

Palmer, M, Nevell, M and Sissons, M, 2012 *Industrial Archaeology: A Handbook.* York: Council for British Archaeology

Patterson, B, 1989 *Give'er a Cheer Boys: The Great Docks of Portsmouth Dockyard.* Portsmouth Royal Dockyard Historical Society Paper **5**

Perren, R, 1995 *Agriculture in Depression, 1870–1940.* Cambridge: Cambridge University Press

Pile, F, 1949 *Ack-Ack Britain's defence against air attack during the Second World War.* London: Harrap

Pratt, E A, 1921 *British Railways and the Great War.* London: Selwyn and Blount Ltd, 2 vols. Available at Cornell University Library: https://archive.org/details/cu31924092566136. Accessed 3 March 2015

Priestley, R E, 1921 *The Signal Service in the European War of 1914 to 1918 (France)*. 1st edn Chatham: W & J Mackay & Co Ltd

Pritchard, T W, 2002 *A History of the Old Parish of Hawarden*. Wrexham: Bridge Books

Rae, J, 1970 *Conscience and Politics: The British Government and the Conscientious Objector to Military Service 1916–1919*. London: Oxford University Press

Reynolds, D, 2013 *The Long Shadow The Great War and the twentieth century*. London: Simon & Schuster

Riley, R, 1985 The Evolution of the Docks and Industrial Buildings in Portsmouth Royal Dockyard 1698–1914, *Portsmouth Papers* **44**

Rodger, R (ed), 1989 *Scottish Housing in the Twentieth Century*. Leicester: Leicester University Press

Sassoon, S, 1930 *Memoirs of an Infantry Officer*. London: Faber & Faber

Saunders, A, 1989 *Fortress Britain: Artillery fortifications in the British Isles and Ireland*. Liphook: Beaufort

Saunders, N J, 2010 *Killing time: Archaeology and the First World War* (revised edn). Stroud: The History Press

Saunders, N, Schofield, J and Glass, E, 2014 The Home Front (1914–1918) and its Legacies: A pilot study for national public archaeology recording project of First World War legacies in Britain: 2014–2018; typescript report for English Heritage. Available at: https://www.historicengland.org.uk/images-books/publications/home-front-1914-1918-and-its-legacies/. Accessed 7 April 2015

Seton Hutchinson, G, 1938 *Machine guns: their history and tactical employment (being also a history of the machine gun corps, 1916–1922)* London: Macmillan

Simkin, P, 2007 *Kitchener's Army, the Raising of the New Armies 1914–1916*. Barnsley: Pen & Sword

Skinner, R, 2011 *Kitchener's Camp at Seaford, a First World War Landscape on Aerial Photographs*. Available at: http://research.historicengland.org.uk/Report.aspx?i=14979&ru=%2fResults.aspx%3fp%3d1%26n%3d10%26a%3d4656%26ns%3d1. Accessed 7 April 2015

Smith, V, 2014 'Barbed Wire Island': Sheppey and the Defended Ports of the Thames and Medway during the First World War, *Fort* **42**, 141–75

Smith, V, Anstee, A and Mason, S, 2014 Britain's First World War defences, *After the Battle* **165**, 39–49

Sockett, E W, 1989 Yorkshire's early warning system, 1916–1936, *Yorkshire Archaeological Journal* **61**, 181–8

Stell, G P, 2011 *Orkney at War: Defending Scapa Flow: vol 1, World War I*. Kirkwall: Orcadian

Stepple, G A, 1992 *Britons, To Arms! The Story of the British Volunteer Soldier*. Stroud: Alan Sutton Publishing Ltd

Stratton, M, and Trinder, B, 2000 *Twentieth Century Industrial Archaeology*. London: E & F N Spon

Swenarton, M, 1981 *Homes fit for Heroes: The politics and architecture of early state housing in Britain*. London: Heinemann

Todman, D, 2005 *The Great War: myth and memory*. London: Hambledon and London

Ullathorne, H, 2006 *Training Trenches at Redmires Sheffield, The Great War Remembered*. Sheffield: University of Sheffield. Available at: http://www.pals.org.uk/sheffield/redmires.pdf. Accessed 3 March 2015

Vernon, S, 2003 Westfield Memorial Village, Lancaster – 'one of a kind', *Lancashire Local Historian* **16**

Way, T, 2008 *Allotments*. Princes Risborough: Shire Publications

West, N, 1986 *GCHQ: The Secret Wireless War, 1900–86*. London: Weidenfeld and Nicolson

Wilson, I, 2011 *HMS Drake: Rathlin Island shipwreck*. Rathlin Island: Rathlin Island Books

Winter, J, 1995 *Sites of Memory, Sites of Mourning: the Great War in European Cultural History*. Cambridge: Cambridge University Press

Yarnall, J, 2011 *Barbed wire disease: British & German Prisoners of War, 1914–19*. Stroud: The History Press

Index

Entries in **bold** refer to the illustrations